P9-CBX-702

Evangelism on the Cutting Edge is a collection of essays that confront the major issues that are hindering the work of fulfilling Christ's mandate to preach the gospel and make disciples of all nations. Written by professors associated with the Trinity Evangelical Divinity School, each of these essays gives a perceptive analysis and biblical response to a specific area of concern:

- *how universalism and religious pluralism sabotage the doctrine of salvation through Christ alone*
- *ecumenicalism and the erosion of the gospel's biblical and historical meaning*
- *the necessity of the authority and inerrancy of Scripture for spiritual awakening and revival*
- *responding to the cry for social justice with the transforming power of the gospel*
- *the benefits and dangers of contextualizing the Bible to make the gospel meaningful to all cultures*
- *encountering demonic forces through the power of prayer and God's intervention*
- *a Christian approach to the self-worshiping, antireligious extremes of secular psychology*
- *homiletic considerations in calling for decisions for Christ*
- *making disciples–the oft-neglected part of the Great Commission*
- *returning discipleship and evangelism as the heart and purpose of all theological training*

These essays will give you a renewed sense of urgency and concern for proclaiming the gospel of our crucified and risen Savior and making disciples for His service.

Other Books by Robert E. Coleman

Established by the Word
Introducing the Prayer Cell
Life in the Living Word
The Master Plan of Evangelism
The Spirit and the Word
Dry Bones Can Live Again
One Divine Moment (*Editor*)
Written in Blood
Evangelism in Perspective
The Mind of the Master
They Meet the Master
Songs of Heaven
Growing in the Word
The New Covenant
The Heartbeat of Evangelism
Evangelism on the Cutting Edge (*Editor*)

Evangelism
on the
Cutting Edge

Edited by
Dr. Robert E. Coleman

Power Books
Fleming H. Revell Company
Old Tappan, New Jersey

Unless otherwise identified, Scripture quotations are from the King James Version of the Bible.

Scripture quotations identified NIV taken from the HOLY BIBLE: NEW INTERNATIONAL VERSION. Copyright © 1973, 1978 by the International Bible Society. Used by permission of Zondervan Bible Publishers.

Scripture quotations identified NAS are from the New American Standard Bible, © The Lockman Foundation 1960, 1962, 1963, 1968, 1971, 1972, 1973, 1975, 1977.

Scripture quotations in this publication identified NKJV are from The New King James Version. Copyright © 1979, 1980, 1982 Thomas Nelson, Inc., Publishers.

Scripture quotations identified AT are the author's translation.

Library of Congress Cataloging-in-Publication Data
Main entry under title:

Evangelism on the cutting edge.

    Includes bibliographical references.
    1. Evangelistic work—Addresses, essays, lectures.
I. Coleman, Robert Emerson, 1928–   .
BV3795.E92   1986   269'.2   85-28281
ISBN 0-8007-1482-2
ISBN 0-8007-5222-8 (pbk.)

Copyright © 1986 by Robert E. Coleman
Published by Fleming H. Revell Company
Old Tappan, New Jersey 07675
All rights reserved
Printed in the United States of America

Contents

Introduction

Getting on Course

Abraham Lincoln is reported to have said: "If we could first know where we are and whither we are heading, we could better judge what to do and how to do it."

The wisdom of these words certainly applies to the work of evangelism—bringing sinners to know the crucified and risen Savior, the only Redeemer of the world, and to serve Him as Lord in the fellowship of the church.[1] Every person who believes in Christ lives under the mandate to announce the good news to the ends of the earth, looking toward the day when His people will be gathered from every tongue and tribe and nation to praise Him forever.

Yet we are far from this objective today. Those who evaluate the progress of church growth tell us that there are 400 million more people in the world now without the Word of life than there were thirty years ago. This is the case despite the increased number of people professing to follow the Savior. In fact, if the present trend of church growth continues, considering the projected increase in population, there will be more unevangelized people by the end of this century than there are persons living on earth today.[2]

---

[1] This definition is adapted from "The Berlin Statement" issued by the World Congress on Evangelism in Berlin, Germany, 1966. The complete statement reads: "Evangelism is the proclamation of the Gospel of the crucified and risen Christ, the only Redeemer of men, according to the Scriptures, with the purpose of persuading condemned and lost sinners to put their trust in God by receiving and accepting Christ as Saviour through the power of the Holy Spirit, and to serve Christ as Lord in every calling of life in the fellowship of His Church, looking toward the day of His coming in glory."

[2] These projections are computed from figures of the Lausanne Committee for World Evangelization, in the release, "Let the Earth Hear His Voice"; also the *IFMA News,* published by Interdenominational Foreign Missions Association, Wheaton, Illinois, 1984, vol. 35, no. 2, p. 4. For a comprehensive treatment of the situation, both the decline of Christianity's proportion of adherents to the

Clearly something must be done to accelerate the evangelistic outreach of the church. While there is much to be excited about regarding the wider penetration of the gospel witness, overall we are falling behind our goal every day. We must recognize where we are, honestly face the problems, and endeavor to align our way with the course God has set for us.

Plan of the Book

That is the purpose of this book. It seeks to clarify our focus concerning issues critical to evangelism in our day. How we deal with them will greatly influence the movement of the church in the years to come. Not every concern can be addressed, of course. The length of this volume naturally limits the selection. But the subjects which are chosen, on balance, provide a good insight to the cutting edge in the contemporary evangelism debate.

Distinguished theologian Dr. Kenneth Kantzer begins the presentation by lifting up the revelation of Jesus Christ, the only name given unto men whereby a hopelessly fallen race must be saved. Yet he observes how in many quarters of the world evangelization is being sabotaged through forms of religious pluralism. This doctrinal erosion can be seen especially in the Conciliar Movement, Protestant and Catholic, a trend traced by Dr. Arthur Johnston, eminent ecumenical observer. At stake is the biblical and historical meaning of the gospel, which, in turn, is bound up with the regard one has for the holy Scriptures, both in terms of the Bible's inerrant witness and the demands it makes upon our lives. Relating this issue to revival, church historian Dr. Wayne Detzler shows how disbelief in the Bible undermines evangelism and brings moral dissolution. Conversely, obedience to the Bible leads to spiritual awakening, both individually and in the corporate life of a people.

But what about the oppression and entrenched evil in society? Speaking to this burning question, particularly heard from the un-

---

world's population and the phenomenal expansion of the church's witness in this century, see the *World Christian Encyclopedia,* edited by David B. Barrett (Oxford: Oxford University Press, 1982), esp. pp. 3–19.

derdeveloped nations, Dr. William Taylor examines the cry for social justice and liberation, and what it portends for the witness of the church. His many years of service as a missionary in Latin America give him a special sensitivity to the problem. Turning then to the challenge of culture to effective evangelism, Dr. David Hesselgrave shows the necessity of contextualizing the message. With keen insight, this veteran missiologist considers both negative and positive aspects of the responsibility, keeping always in view the authority of biblical truth.

The struggle against demonic power is still another dimension of the real world we live in. Meeting it head-on, missionary educator Dr. Timothy Warner describes the conflict between light and darkness, emphasizing the place of prayer and divine intervention in battling principalities and spiritual wickedness. From a completely different vantage point, psychologist Dr. Gary Collins treats the new, man-made religion of psychology, which, in its pure, naturalistic form, eliminates any need for belief in supernatural grace or redemption from sin. Instead, self-determination and personal fulfillment take the place of salvation by faith in the Son of God.

No compilation on evangelism would be adequate without some contribution on preaching. So to lift up this crucial ministry, Dr. Lloyd Perry, renowned homiletician of two generations, writes on the call for decision, and he offers some helpful counsel on giving the invitation. Paralleling the mandate to preach the gospel and giving it direction, is our Lord's command to make disciples of all nations. Dr. Robert E. Coleman develops this theme, stressing that the Great Commission is not a special gift or calling, but a life-style incumbent upon every follower of Christ.

This should be nowhere more evident than in schools involved with the training of leaders for the church. That this is not always the case is painfully apparent. With this burden on his heart, Dr. Walter Kaiser, Jr., esteemed seminary dean, urges that Christ's discipling mandate become the controlling purpose of all theological education—a fitting conclusion to the series.

All the authors are in relationship with the teaching faculty at Trinity Evangelical Divinity School. Though sharing a common commitment to evangelism, each writes from his own unique perspective. The variety of the essays adds color and depth to the collection.

Use of the Content

The book is intended for general reading and discussion. Each author raises an important matter, though certainly not the last word on the subject. Some persons, doubtless, will disagree with viewpoints expressed. But it is hoped that the forthright presentations will stimulate inquiry. To aid in this process, a few questions for thought follow the chapters.

By concentrating upon principles, not techniques or programs, considerable room is left for filling in details. The reader is encouraged to do this, finding specific applications in his or her own situation. In this practical area there is plenty of opportunity for creative realism.

Though the writers have worked within strict guidelines of brevity, they have tried to be fair and objective in their assessment of the issues. Each has attempted to document sources and, also, to indicate where additional material may be found. The serious student wanting more information will find these references helpful.

The Ultimate Goal

It is hoped that reflection on these themes will sharpen the reader's understanding and appreciation of the global task before us. To be sure, there are many dangerous cross-currents and undertows surging beneath the surface of the Christian mission. But the ultimate triumph of the gospel is never in doubt. That is the certainty which puts a song in our hearts.

I am reminded of a letter General William Booth of the Salvation Army wrote his daughter at a time in her life when she was going through great discouragement. As a loving father can do, he admonished her to take her eyes off the waves and fix them on the tide.

That would be good advice for us, as well. However tumultuous the present conditions may appear, we must not be distracted by the passing whims of human fancy; rather let us fix our gaze upon the unchanging nature of God's eternal purpose. Someday the Great Commission will be fulfilled, Jesus Christ will reign as Lord of all, and to Him every knee shall bow. Evangelism ever keeps this destiny in view.

If this book in any small measure can help someone sort out the temporary fads from the permanent realities, and get with the action of God's Spirit in the world, then it will have accomplished its design.

Evangelism
on the
Cutting
Edge

1

The Claims of Christ and Religious Pluralism

Kenneth S. Kantzer

Kenneth S. Kantzer is Dean Emeritus and Distinguished Professor of Biblical and Systematic Theology at Trinity Evangelical Divinity School, and Chancellor of Trinity College. He has been Editor-in-Chief of *Christianity Today,* and still serves as one of the senior editors, as well as Dean of the Christianity Today Institute.

He received the B.A. degree from Ashland (Ohio) College, the M.A. from Ohio State University, the B.D. and S.T.M. from Faith Theological Seminary. In addition, he holds the Ph.D. in philosophy and religion from Harvard University, and spent a year of post-doctoral study at the University of Goettingen in Germany and the University of Basel in Switzerland.

Before coming to Trinity Evangelical Divinity School in 1963, he was for many years Chairman of the Division of Bible, Philosophy and Christian Education at Wheaton College. For a short time he held a pastorate in Rockport, Massachusetts, and has served as an ordained minister in the Evangelical Free Church of America since 1950. Dr. Kantzer also taught at Gordon College and Divinity School as well as the King's College.

Dr. Kantzer is a member of the American Theological Society and of the Evangelical Theological Society, having served as president of the latter organization. In addition to numerous articles in major religious journals, he has written chapters in *Religions in a Changing World, The Evangelicals, Inspiration and Interpretation, The Word for this Century,* and *Jesus of Nazareth: Savior and Lord.* He has also edited two volumes, *Evangelical Roots* and *Perspectives on Evangelical Theology.*

The Saving Gospel

Christianity, so C. S. Lewis once said, has no message for those who do not realize that they are sinners. According to the Bible the root problem of mankind is sin. In the panoramic view of the human predicament set forth in his epistle to the Romans, the Apostle Paul declares: "All have sinned and come short of the glory of God" (Romans 3:23); and "The wages of sin is death" (Romans 6:23).

Yet God did not choose to leave man in his lostness. Notwithstanding the divine judgment upon all men because of their wickedness, God loves every human being (Romans 5:8). By means of the gospel He offers to all a way of forgiveness and reconciliation that does not do violence to His holiness and justice (Romans 3:26).

In the Old Testament God promised salvation through a redeemer to come (Genesis 3:15). In the New Testament that promised remedy for man's lostness is to be found in Jesus, the Messiah. In Him sinful man can find reconciliation with the holy God. "For God so loved the world, that he gave his only begotten Son, that whosoever believeth in him should not perish but have everlasting life" (John 3:16).

The good news of what Jesus Christ has done for sinners and offers to them freely on the sole condition of repentance and faith must be carried to every creature (Mark 16:15; 1 Corinthians 9:16). The gospel is God's remedy for the human predicament—the only hope of humankind. "And this is the record, that God hath given us eternal life and this life is in his Son. He that hath the Son hath life and he that hath not the Son of God hath not life" (1 John 5:11–12).

Down through two millennia the lostness of humankind without Christ has been the greatest impetus for the worldwide mission program of the Christian church. The Apostle Paul summarizes this missionary imperative in the tenth chapter of Romans:

> For whoever will call upon the name of the Lord will be saved. How then shall they call upon Him in whom they have not believed? And how shall they believe in Him

whom they have not heard? And how shall they hear
without a preacher? And how shall they preach unless
they are sent. . . ? So faith comes from hearing, and hearing by the word of Christ.

Romans 10:13, 17 NAS

The Liberal Reconstruction of the Missionary Task

Yet, the terrible thought of the lostness of mankind without Jesus
Christ has led all but those who take the biblical record seriously to
move to a more moderate position. Traditional liberalism, for example, not only denied the full deity of Jesus Christ but also tended
to follow the leadership of Friedrich Schleiermacher who argued
for the universal salvation of all humans. For most liberals Christianity is not the unique, divinely approved remedy for the human
predicament. It is only the highest and best revelation of the character and will of God. Other religions are by no means bereft of divine
revelation; and they, too, can nurture mankind in redemptive ways.

Classic expression was given to the liberal position by William
Ernest Hocking in the volume *Rethinking Missions: A Layman's Inquiry after One Hundred Years*.[1] Incidentally, the one hundred years
represented almost to the day the century immediately following
the work of Friedrich Schleiermacher, the father of modern liberalism, who flourished in the early part of the nineteenth century.[2]

The essential thrust of Hocking's not-so-new liberal approach to
missions represented a 180-degree turn in mission strategy from the
previous history of the church in both its Catholic and Evangelical
branches. Representing generally the liberal position, Hocking ar-

---

[1] William Ernest Hocking, *Rethinking Missions* (New York: Harper & Bros.,
1932).

[2] Hocking's thesis was by no means new even on the American scene. The
thesis of his *Inquiry* was commonly accepted in Germany through the nineteenth century. In America the same broad view was widely held among the in-
telligentsia. Note, for example, the literary theme of the "noble savage." James
Fenimore Cooper expressed this view clearly through his character Natty
Bumppo, in *The Leatherstocking Tales*. His *Deerslayer* (c. 1841) and *Last of the
Mohicans* (c. 1826) were part of the basic reading for generations of Americans
through the nineteenth and twentieth centuries. What was new in Hocking's *Inquiry* is that it set forth this broader view as a clear conviction of a large segment
of the leadership in traditionally Protestant and Evangelical churches.

gued that the task of missions should not be to convert the heathen from their various ethnic religions. Rather, the goal of missions should be to help a Muslim or Hindu or Buddhist be a better representative of his own religion. Each religious tradition can learn from the other. While Christianity may be the best of all religions, it shares the good with other religions and needs to learn from them as well as to share with them.

More recently, Arnold Toynbee, the world-renowned Anglican philosopher of history, represents the same point of view. He states:

> Since self-centeredness is innate in human nature, we are all inclined, to some extent, to assume that our own religion is the only true and right religion; . . . while the rest of the human race are Gentiles sitting in darkness. Such pride and prejudice are symptoms of original sin.[3]

The five higher religions—Buddhism, Hinduism, Judaism, Islam and Christianity, but especially Islam, Judaism, and Christianity—should seek to join forces in order to strengthen the cause of those who stand for religious values in the modern world.[4] It is imperative, therefore, he concludes, that "One ought . . . to try to purge our Christianity of the traditional western belief that Christianity is unique."[5]

Bishop J. A. T. Robinson became, perhaps, the most vocal, if not most respected, of modern voices trumpeting a similar view from his position as a responsible leader of the church. He argued that all human beings of good will are, in fact, implicit believers. The church, therefore, should carry on its work as a cooperative effort even with atheists and agnostics, who are, albeit unconsciously, Christian in spite of themselves.[6]

Liberal theologian John Hick, an English Presbyterian, likewise insists that all great religions bring people equally into a valid en-

---

[3] Arnold Toynbee, *An Historian's Approach to Religion* (New York: Oxford University Press, 1979), p. 301.
[4] Ibid., p. 256.
[5] Arnold Toynbee, *Christianity Among the Religions of the World* (New York: Scribner, 1957), p. 95.
[6] John A. T. Robinson, *Honest to God* (London: SCM, 1963), p. 55 *et passim.*

counter with God. He argues, as had Hocking before him, that to seek to convert from one religion to another is the height of provincialism. Rather than uproot the followers of other religions from their cultural moorings, we should join hands with them in our seeking for the good. He adds, "If I had been born in India, I probably would be a Hindu; if in Egypt, probably a Muslim; if in Ceylon, probably a Buddhist; but I was born in England, and am predictably, a Christian."[7]

Growing Religious Pluralism in the World Council

In spite of its most recent emphasis upon biblical piety, illustrated at the World Council meeting in Vancouver of 1983, the leadership and official publications of the World Council of Churches have increasingly moved in support of the liberal position. They have failed to diagnose the fundamental predicament of mankind as human sin that separates man from a holy God and rightly calls forth divine judgment. Consequently all too often they see no need of the biblical gospel as the remedy for man's dire predicament.

In the World Council of Churches' study volume prepared for the Vancouver Assembly, John Paulton lists as one *unlikely* option that "only those calling upon Jesus as their personal Savior can be saved, the rest of humanity being assigned to eternal perdition."[8] Religious pluralism that places all religions basically on the same level is the theological corollary of this view.

The Vancouver theme, "Jesus Christ the Hope of the World," could be interpreted as a rejection of syncretism; but it was not so interpreted by the World Council in its official preassembly study guide.

In the end the great communities of faith will not have disappeared. None will have "won" over the others. Jews will still be Jews; Muslims still Muslims; and those of the

---

[7] John Hick, "The Reconstruction of Christian Belief for Today and Tomorrow," *Theology* (Sept., 1970), p. 399.

[8] *Christianity Today* (April 20, 1984), Vol. 28, No. 27, p. 12.

great Eastern faiths, still Buddhists or Hindus or Taoists. Africa will still witness to its traditional life view; China to its inheritance. People will still come from the East and the West, the North and the South, and sit down in the kingdom of God, without having first become "Christians" like us.[9]

All religions apparently lead to God; Jesus Christ, is merely *our* way.

At Vancouver this growing syncretism gained further support from the Indian mythology employed in worship, from the role given to the leaders of other religions, and from the stern warning presented by World Council official D. C. Mulder *against* evangelizing because it imposed an obstacle to dialogue with other religions.[10]

Not surprisingly, the liberal denial of the uniqueness of the Christian message and its necessity for personal salvation has had devastating effects upon the mission staffs of the world.

Perhaps the best way to show how dramatic the missionary retreat has been is to look at the percentage decline in the number of overseas missionaries among some of the major denominations between 1962 and 1979: Episcopal Church, 79 percent decline; Lutheran Church of America, 70 percent; United Presbyterian Church in the U.S.A., 72 percent; United Church of Christ, 68 percent; Christian Church Disciples, 66 percent; United Methodist Church, 46 percent; American Lutheran Church, 44 percent.[11]

Though many factors contributed to this decline, it is legitimate to reckon that these figures are a rough index of the depth of conviction about basic Christian doctrine—the nature of the gospel, the lostness of mankind apart from Christ, and the necessity of obeying

---

[9] Ibid.
[10] Ibid.
[11] Ibid. (Sept. 19, 1981), Vol. 25, No. 16, p. 16.

biblical mandates calling for sacrifice and discipline for the sake of advancing the kingdom of Christ.[12]

The Universalism of Neoorthodoxy

In the middle years of the twentieth century, the movement called Neoorthodoxy flourished first on the continent of Europe and then later in North America. Its foremost representative, Karl Barth, sought to retain a basically supernatural Christianity along with large elements of historical criticism carried over from the liberalism of the post-enlightenment era. Against liberalism, he spoke out strongly against the possibility of knowing God on the basis of any general revelation[13] or immediate awareness of God apart from Christ.[14] Accordingly, he judged all ethnic religions very harshly: "The god of Mohammed is an idol like all other idols."[15]

Yet on the matter of the unique necessity of the Christian message and the lostness of mankind without Christ, Karl Barth followed almost exactly in the steps of his liberal predecessor of a century before—Friedrich Schleiermacher. Like Schleiermacher, he argued for a divine predestination of all human beings to salvation. Without quite committing himself absolutely to universalism, he could accordingly be described as a hope-so universalist. The purpose of the mission task is not to enable lost men to be saved but to inform them that they have already been saved by Jesus Christ.[16]

In recent years Barth's influence has waned significantly, both on the Continent and in North America. And even in its heyday, Neoorthodoxy did little to stem the shrinking of missionary forces. The mission task for them, too, was no longer to bring lost and dying men into eternal life through Jesus Christ the Savior, but

[12] Ibid.

[13] Karl Barth, "No!" in Karl Barth and Emil Brunner, *Natural Theology* (London: Geoffrey Bles, 1946), pp. 58–60.

[14] Karl Barth, *Church Dogmatics* (Edinburgh: T. and T. Clark, 1956), Vol. I, pt. 2, pp. 300 ff.

[15] Karl Barth, *The Knowledge of God and the Service of God* (London: Hodder and Stoughton, 1938), p. 21.

[16] Karl Barth, *Church Dogmatics*, Vol. IV, pt. 1, 164 *et passim*. See also G. C. Berkouwer, *The Triumph of Grace in the Theology of Karl Barth* (Grand Rapids: Eerdmans, 1956), pp. 292 to 296.

rather to bring those who had already been redeemed to an awareness of that happy conclusion of which they were assured—even
though they did not know it.

The Liberalizing of Roman Catholicism

Roman Catholicism, which had stood so firmly during the first
half of the twentieth century for the uniqueness of the gospel and
the necessity of a right relationship to God only through the Roman
Church, quickly thereafter experienced a drastic revision of its former stance.[17] The greatest of the Roman Catholic theologians, Mu-
nich professor Karl Rahner, held forth wide hope for salvation
outside the church. In "Christianity and the Non-Christian Religions," Rahner argued for the existence of "anonymous Christianity."

> The pagan, after the beginning of the Christian mission,
> who lives in the state of Christ's grace through faith, hope
> and love, yet who has no explicit knowledge of the fact . . .
> is oriented in grace-given salvation to Jesus Christ.[18]

With this understanding of salvation experiences for the followers of non-Christian religions, Rahner then explains his understanding of the purpose of the church mission. "The proclamation
of the gospel does not simply turn someone absolutely abandoned
by God and Christ into a Christian, but turns an anonymous
Christian into someone who now also knows about his Christian
belief . . ."[19]

A slightly more radical approach to the issue has been provided
by Hans Küng. He objected to Rahner's labeling of those who were
saved outside the boundaries of the visible Roman church as "se-

[17] See David Wells, *Revolution in Rome* (Downers Grove, Ill.: Inter-Varsity
Press, 1972).
[18] Karl Rahner, *Theological Investigations,* 14 Vols. (New York: Seabury
Press, 1974 to 1976), Vol. 5 pp. 115 *ff.*; and Vol. 14, p. 283.
[19] Karl Rahner, "Christianity and the Non-Christian Religions," in *Theological Investigations,* Vol. V, p. 132.

cret" or "anonymous" Christians. In his view all major religions are valid to lead to salvation. Non-Christian religions, in fact, represent the "normal" and "ordinary" means of salvation. Since everyone is saved by divine grace, it is clear that the vast majority do not attain salvation through the Christian church and its witness but through the mediation of non-Christian religions. Non-Christian religions, therefore, must be recognized as legitimate "ways" of salvation.[20]

What sense does it make then, Küng asks of Karl Rahner, to call a godly Muslim or a devout Buddhist an "anonymous Christian?" Since the practice of their non-Christian religion is the means through which the divine grace was mediated to them, it is sheer arrogance to call them secret or anonymous Christians.[21]

Hans Küng summarizes his view as follows:

> We can be glad that God's grace, as it is revealed to us in Christ, is so vast and wide that it embraces the whole world; all men are within His good pleasure. We can be glad that we do not need to condemn any of these pagans in Asia or Africa or in the middle of Europe. As witnesses to the faith and apostles of Jesus Christ, we may and should proclaim the gospel to them, in the knowledge that God's grace in Jesus Christ has already reached to embrace them.[22]

Since Vatican II broader views like those of Rahner and Küng have led most Roman Catholic scholars (though not the masses of the church's members) to views that are scarcely distinguishable from liberal Protestantism. And the effect on Roman Catholic missions has been devastating. Maryknoll (Glen Ellyn, Ill.) Seminary for the training of missionaries has closed its doors; and many Roman Catholic missionaries, especially those in South America, have identified with the Marxist "Liberation Theology," according to which the task of the church is not primarily to bring those who

---

[20] Hans Küng, *On Being a Christian* (Garden City, N.Y.: Doubleday, 1976), p. 91.

[21] Ibid.; and *see also That the World May Believe.* (N.Y.: Sheed and Ward, 1963), p. 117 *et passim.*

[22] *That the World May Believe,* p. 117.

stand under the judgment of God into a knowledge of Christ and eternal life through Him, but rather to encourage them to find freedom from oppression in this life.[23]

The "Cosmic Christ" of Some Evangelicals

Evangelicals have not proved immune to the pressures of liberalism that would erode the doctrine of man's lostness. Yet it is only fair to say that, at least as yet, it has not destroyed or even noticeably lessened their historic motivation for the missionary task.

In the early years of the twentieth century, Baptist theologian A. H. Strong argued for salvation through the "Cosmic Christ." On the basis of Acts 10:34–35 and related texts, he argued that those who never heard the gospel can be saved. "So the heathen who casts himself upon God's mercy, may receive salvation from the Crucified One, without knowing who is the giver, or that the gift was purchased by agony and blood."[24]

As an Evangelical, however, Strong insisted that the heathen could be saved (1) only on the basis of the atoning work of Jesus Christ, (2) only on the condition of repentance and faith, and (3) only on the condition of personal trust in Jesus Christ, the divine Lord and Savior.

Strong quickly reassures his readers, however, that "The number of such is so small as in no degree to weaken the claims of the missionary enterprise upon us."[25] Yet, even so, in some few cases, these conditions could be met by those who had never heard of the historical incarnation and atonement and resurrection of Christ. By special revelation we who have the Scriptures know that Jesus Christ is God incarnate, and that it is He alone who can redeem us. Yet by the electing grace of God working through His Holy Spirit, non-Christians can exercise saving faith. Their faith, then, would be in

---

[23] Gustavo Gutiérrez, *A Theology of Liberation* (Maryknoll, New York: Orbis, 1973), p. 10 *et passim.*

[24] Augustus Hopkins Strong, *Systematic Theology*, 3 Vols. (Valley Forge, PA: The Judson Press, 1907), p. 843.

[25] Ibid.

that same incarnate God but without the knowledge that He had become incarnate.[26]

At a Wheaton consultation in April, 1985, Clark Pinnock, Professor of Systematic Theology at McMaster University, presented a similar point of view.[27] This position had been elaborated and defended at the turn of the century by William G. T. Shedd, who cited numerous Evangelicals and near-Evangelicals from the ancient church as well as in Reformation times who espoused a broader understanding of salvation apart from the knowledge of the historic gospel.[28]

Evangelical Cautions

Generally, however, the Reformation churches and their Evangelical successors were, on biblical grounds, very wary of holding out much hope for the broader view of personal salvation. The Westminster Confession states: "Men not professing the Christian religion cannot be saved in any other way whatever, be they never so diligent to frame their lives according to the light of nature and the law of that religion which they do profess" (X, 4).

Similarly, the Anglican Thirty-nine Articles, in article 18, warns:

> They also are to be accursed that presume to say, that every man shall be saved by the law or sect which he professeth so that he be diligent to frame his life according to the law, and the light of nature. For Holy Scripture doth set out unto us only the name of Jesus Christ, whereby men must be saved.

Yet Evangelicals are likewise unwilling to lay down boundaries as to how God must perform His work in the hearts of men. The

---

[26] Ibid., pp. 23, 574, 843, and especially his *Christ in Creation and Ethical Monism* (Philadelphia: The Griffith and Roland Press, 1899).

[27] "Leading Evangelical Scholars Trade their Latest Insights" in *Christianity Today* (April 19, 1985) Vol. 29, No. 7, pp. 56–57.

[28] William G. T. Shedd, *Dogmatic Theology*, 2 Vols. (Grand Rapids: Zondervan, 1891–1894), Vol. II, pp. 704–714.

Westminster Confession (X,3) also states, "Elect infants dying in infancy are regenerated and saved by Christ through the Spirit, who worketh when and where and how He pleaseth." The Confession then adds, "So also are all other elect persons who are incapable of being outwardly called by the ministry of the Word" (X,3). While this was, no doubt, mainly intended as a reference to idiots and insane persons, it may also indicate that on rare occasions God is pleased to regenerate without the use of the written revelation. Such biblical characters as Jethro, Melchizedek, and Balaam have always posed questions unanswered by the Scriptures as to how these individuals outside the mainstream of the visible people of God came to a knowledge of redemption.

Acts 10:34–35 certainly teaches that God in His grace works in the hearts of those who have never been touched by the gospel message and does so with the intent of leading them to salvation. For example Cornelius is set up as a type of *those from every nation* who fear God and do what is right. The apostle recognizes him not as a proselyte who has accepted the revelation of redemption offered. Rather he views Cornelius as a pagan who has responded to the much dimmer light of nature and conscience. He is in the same category of those of whom the Apostle Paul speaks in Acts 17:27 (NAS) they "seek after God, if perhaps they might . . . find Him." But in Cornelius' case, the important factor is that he did respond to the light available to those from every nation.

The general biblical principle is that God has provided for all men a witness to Himself in creation (Romans 1:18 ff) and in conscience (Romans 2:14–15). In addition, He has sent His Spirit to convince the world of sin and of the need for divine forgiveness (John 16:8–11). And the Scriptures promise us that he who truly seeks will surely find (Revelation 3:20; Matthew 7:7; Luke 11:9).

No doubt Strong and those who follow him are on the right track. The redemptive activity of God is wider than the boundaries of the historical gospel. Yet the Bible is abundantly clear that no one is saved on the basis of his obedience to the revelation in creation or the moral law or conscience. Rather the law condemns, because all men, apart from Christ, have failed to obey the good that they know (Romans 3:23). If anyone is ever saved, therefore, it can only be on the basis of the atoning work of Christ and on condition of faith in Christ (Romans 3:25–26).

While recognizing the elements of truth in the position of Strong, therefore, many, perhaps most, Evangelicals have understood such Scriptures to indicate that there is no biblical salvation without a knowledge of the biblical gospel. God works in the hearts of all men to draw them to Himself (John 1:8). Anyone, anytime and anywhere, who recognizes his or her sin and rests upon the mercy of God will be "acceptable" to God. But God's method of saving the person will be through the gospel.

No one questions what God could do. In mysterious matters of the human soul, however, we can only be guided by His Word of revelation. And that divine Word seems to tie what the Bible means by salvation very tightly to the preaching of the gospel.

Does God employ extraordinary means, beyond the normal human preaching of the gospel, to bring the message of Christ to those whom He has prepared to receive it? Surely we have no right to say that God could not bring Christ to a repentant sinner by a miracle or vision or by any other means He chooses.

Yet the Scriptures certainly lay great stress on the knowledge of the gospel and on the crucial role of the church in bearing witness to the Savior. Conversely, the Bible holds out little hope of human salvation for those who have never heard the gospel.

Even the Cornelius paradigm, though on the surface it may seem to offer strong support for Strong's view, on more careful analysis falls unequivocally on the other side. The text states explicitly that Cornelius was not "saved" until after he had received the gospel message. As the text records it: "And he [Peter] shall speak words to you by which you will be saved" (Acts 11:14 NAS).

The Apostle John, likewise, points specifically to the *name* of the Savior: "He who does not believe has been judged already, because he has not believed in the name of the only begotten Son of God" (John 3:18 NAS). In similar fashion, the Apostle Peter declares: "There is no other name under heaven that has been given among men, by which we must be saved" (Acts 4:12 NAS).

And the whole point of the Apostle Paul in Romans 10:11, 12 is the necessity of hearing the message and upon our responsibility as believers to bear witness to the gospel. If salvation is only through Jesus, if He is truly the one way to a right relationship to God, that lays an awesome responsibility upon all who believe to bend every possible effort to share this good news with all men and women everywhere.

"Without Christ," the Apostle warns us in his epistle to the Ephesians (*see* 2:12), we are "without God" and "without hope." This dreadful truth of the lostness of humankind without Christ is the dark side of the biblical message. But the good news is that God is not willing that any should perish (2 Peter 3:9). He has gone to infinite lengths to win us back to Himself. And this in turn lays an immense responsibility on all who love God and seek to obey His command to share this good news with all people everywhere. If God has other means besides our Christian witness to communicate the gospel, He does not encourage us to rely upon them. Rather, He calls upon every Christian to take up this task with utmost seriousness. If we love God and love our neighbor, we can do no less. A lost and dying world constrains us to be faithful to our Lord and at all costs to carry forward the mission of the church to preach the gospel to every human being.

Questions for Thought

1. Why do Christians share their knowledge of Christ with others?

2. Since Christ commanded His followers to share their faith with others, is not His command all we need to support a strong missionary movement? Why?

3. How has Roman Catholic missionary strategy changed in the last quarter century?

4. Neoorthodoxy tries to pull the best out of the older Evangelicalism and the new liberalism. Do you think it succeeds? What is the effect upon evangelism?

5. How does A. H. Strong harmonize his view of salvation through Christ alone with his belief that many are saved who have never heard of Christ?

6. What encouragement, if any, do the Scriptures give us to warrant our trusting that humans can be saved without hearing about Christ?

2

Church Unity and the Mission of the Church

Arthur P. Johnston

Arthur P. Johnston, Professor of Mission and Director of the Paul E. Little Chair of Evangelism in the School of World Mission and Evangelism at Trinity Evangelical Divinity School, presently is on leave to serve as President of Tyndale Theological Seminary in Amsterdam, Holland. He holds a bachelor's degree from Wheaton College and an M.A. from Wheaton Graduate School. Further study was done at Faith Theological Seminary and Ecole des Hautes Etudes, University of Paris. His Ph.D. was earned from the University of Strasbourg, France.

Dr. and Mrs. Johnston established the Evangelical Church of Orly, France, which Dr. Johnston pastored from 1956 to 1967. During part of this time he also taught at Nogent Bible Institute in Paris. He was Chairman of the France Field for the Evangelical Alliance Mission and founding President of the Alliance des Eglises Evangéliques Indépendantes.

A participant in the Berlin Congress on Evangelism in 1966, the Lausanne Congress on World Evangelism in 1974 and the Consultation on World Evangelization in Thailand in 1980, he is a foremost Evangelical spokesman on the world ecumenical movement. For several years he was President of St. Paul Bible College and is a member of the Billy Graham Evangelistic Association.

Dr. Johnston has written two research books entitled *World Evangelism and the Word of God* and *The Battle for World Evangelism.* In addition, he was written articles appearing in numerous Christian magazines.

One in Christ

There can be no doubt that our Lord is concerned about the unity of His people (John 17:20–23). This is something so crucial that Jesus made it congruous to salvation through faith in His Word. A believer does not have any choice. One who receives the finished work of Christ through the Holy Spirit is joined to every other member of the church, and they share together the family character as children of the same heavenly Father (John 17:6–26).[1]

Disunity, however, is also a part of the biblical record in the Old Testament and the New. Israel was to be separate from her neighbors' idolatry and ungodliness. Under the Law she was united under Moses, Joshua, David and others. On the other hand, Israel's idolatry by the worship of the golden calves in the Northern Kingdom brought a disunity between Judah and Israel that lasted over the centuries. Unfaithfulness to their divine calling and written covenant with God ultimately led to exile in Assyria, Babylon and Egypt. In their syncretism with other living faiths the people of God became disunited and separated from their Lord.

The ugly head of disunity appeared even among Jesus' disciples when jealousy arose among them as to who was the greatest. The love of money probably led Judas Iscariot to deny his Lord, leave the disciples and die a horrible death. The faithful disciples, however, were to love one another (John 13:34–35). The common teaching they received from the Lord united them in love. Later on in the apostolic church it was essential that Paul's teaching—his gospel received from the Lord—be confirmed and affirmed by the apostles of Jerusalem (Galatians 2:7–10). The one gospel of Jesus Christ united Peter's evangelization of the Jews and Paul's evangelization of the Gentiles. An evident deviation in doctrine or conduct

---

[1] For helpful treatments of this theme, see "The Nature of Biblical Unity," by Henry Blocher, in *Let the Earth Hear His Voice,* J. D. Douglas, ed. (Minneapolis: World Wide Publications, 1975), pp. 393–99; and the articles by Warren Webster, "The Nature of Church and Unity in Mission," and Wesley L. Deuwel, "Christian Unity: The Biblical Basis and Practical Outgrowth," in *New Horizons in World Mission,* David J. Hesselgrave, ed. (Grand Rapids: Baker, 1979), pp. 243–86.

required discipline or separation (Galatians 1:6–10; 1 Corinthians 5:9–13; Romans 16:17).

The message is straightforward and clear: unity in truth and personal godliness are the solid foundations of world evangelization.

Confusion in Evangelical Ranks

This is not always obvious in Evangelicalism today. As a movement, it possesses those who are moving farther and farther in both theology and in practice away from their fundamental roots. Few Evangelicals of this generation, unfortunately, are aware of the pitched battles our forefathers waged against the erosion of liberalism and modernism in the earlier half of this century. Even less known are the fundamental principles of the sixteenth-century Reformation of the Scriptures alone, grace alone and faith alone. For many, the authority of the historic church is subtly replacing the authority of the Scriptures; liberation for social and political transformation is replacing grace without works; and sociopolitical action is becoming part of the biblical evangelistic message.

An understanding of the current situation requires an overview of the disunity inherited by Evangelicals of this century. The first seven councils of the church (325–787 A.D.) unified the church in Christian doctrine but also separated those who disagreed with their conclusions. In 1054 A.D., a major geographical division occurred between the Eastern (Orthodox) and Western (Roman Catholic) churches. It was attributed to both doctrinal divergencies and personality differences between the leadership of these culturally different churches. Then the Protestant Reformation seriously divided the Roman Catholic Church of Western Europe because of both the doctrinal deviations from the Bible and the moral degeneracy of poorly taught clergy and people.

This century, however, is witnessing one of the most intensive and persistent unity crusades in the history of the Christian church. Beginning with the Evangelical World Missionary Conference at Edinburgh, Scotland, in 1910, the ecumenical movement gathered momentum, eventually bringing into being the World Council of Churches at the First Assembly in Amsterdam in 1948. Although the WCC was composed of Protestant communions, a most notable event took place when the Eastern Orthodox churches joined the WCC in the New Delhi Third Assembly of the WCC in 1961. Events toward church unity have accelerated even more rapidly and dramatically since then.

History of the Decline

Evangelicals are ecumenical by their very nature. They quickly identify with others who are "born of the Spirit" and they affirm readily the new spiritual unity "given" in Christ. One significant dimension of this may be seen in their world missionary efforts in the nineteenth century which brought a "heart unity" beyond the denominational barriers of Protestantism. The Evangelical missionary conferences, beginning at Bombay in 1825, played a significant role in this growing ecumenical council. The organization of the British Evangelical Alliance in 1846 is only one example. Evangelical interdenominational unity was furthered by the great evangelist D. L. Moody, for proclaiming the gospel has always been a common biblical concern of Evangelicals. Youth evangelistic movements, such as the Young Men's Christian Association, also fostered parachurch unity.

Prominent among the early leaders of Protestant ecumenism were John R. Mott and J. H. Oldham. They were nurtured from biblical roots, and developed their leadership abilities in Evangelical youth organizations. Regrettably, as their ministries expanded, some accommodations were made to the liberalizing currents of the time. Desiring ardently to harness the forces of Christianity for world evangelization, one point of Evangelical doctrine after another was surrendered in order to gain the support and cooperation of all Protestant churches. Even before the Edinburgh World Missionary Conference, they solicited the cooperation of the Anglo-Catholics of England, the Eastern Orthodox and the Roman Catholics.

At the Jerusalem 1928 meeting of the newly formed International Missionary Council, the Evangelical roots at Edinburgh were only discernible in a few of the "Old School" Evangelicals who were strongly outnumbered and dominated by the "New School" leadership. The Evangelical evangelistic and missionary mandate was undermined and replaced by an appeal to the social obligation of the church. Missionary efforts were directed toward the establishment of a Christlike world, not toward the evangelism of the world.

The sacrifice of doctrine caused evangelism to suffer and the goal of world evangelization faded. By the Amsterdam assembly of the WCC, gospel outreach began to disappear, and by the New Delhi Assembly it was extinct within the council. Consequently, new associations of Evangelicals arose worldwide to take the places of the formerly Evangelical efforts that had been assimilated into the ecumenical movement.

Rapid Developments in Our Generation

The most dramatic and significant steps toward worldwide Christian unity in history have taken place before our eyes in the last two decades. A primary theological event was the Montreal 1963 meeting of the Faith and Order Commission of the WCC. Also contributing to the unity movement was the Vatican II (1962–65) Council of the Roman Catholic Church which changed the atmosphere of the church from one of confrontation to that of conciliation.

At Montreal the Reformation position of authority in "Scripture alone" shifted to the authority of the "Tradition of the Gospel" as transmitted in the church. Understanding this new viewpoint is crucial, for it means that the authority of the tradition of institutional churches has overshadowed and replaced the authority of the Scriptures. The Bible is part of the flow of tradition, to be sure, but it is not the Bible alone. An official WCC publication states that "the Bible is, as it were, tradition written down at an early stage in its course through the ages."[2] Truth and Christian doctrine, thus, are discerned and determined by a consensus of what the historical churches of Christianity believe. God's written Word has been dethroned. It means that evangelism is in reality a call to faith in the

---

[2] *The Bible, Its Authority and Interpretation in the Ecumenical Movement,* Ellen Flesseman-Van Leer, ed., (Geneva: WCC, 1980), p. 3.

churches who do, however, have the Bible as part of their traditions—an early part of their history.

This view of the Bible in Christian traditions generally is based upon the higher critical view of a fallible scripture. It is not God's inerrant and infallible Scripture by which all doctrine and truth are measured. Evangelism, therefore, cannot be the proclamation of the Bible. It is the proclamation of a church that has the Bible. For many, the Scriptures only represent the way in which God's message was understood by people when the Bible was written. This implies that the biblical message for today varies from culture to culture and from people to people as they individually "do theology": first, people interpret the Bible by getting involved in correcting societal injustices, and then they return to the Bible for their own doctrinal interpretation of their sociopolitical action. There is no one universal gospel message. Evangelicalism, consequently, is one of many Christian approaches to the Bible. Salvation is basically societal, and yet, may be received through faith—faith primarily in the sacraments of an historical church, not in the Christ of the Scriptures. An errant Bible, a cultural interpretation, a societal salvation and a sacramental regeneration results in a pluralism that often denies divine judgment, hell, the blood atonement and heaven, while focusing upon the transformation of society as salvation. Evangelicals will find little in this with which they can identify or should unite.

Vatican II gave Protestants the new status of "separated brethren." Though this nomenclature was less offensive than the anathema pronounced upon Protestants in earlier days, it still left intact the Catholic position of ecclesiastical superiority. However, the new Roman Catholic openness to the Bible and the warm invitation to Protestants to return to the Roman "Mother Church," together with the flexibility of doctrine in the WCC, has clouded the biblical and theological discernment of many Protestant Evangelicals.

Since 1971, the Roman Catholic Church has engaged in individual "conversations" with Anglicans, Disciples of Christ, Lutherans, Reformed, Methodists and Pentecostals. Some of these discussions have included Evangelical leaders. But conversations have their dangers. Vatican II taught that those who have not heard the gospel and yet sincerely seek God will have "life," even though only under the Bishop of Rome in the Roman Catholic Church is found "fullness of life" and the full expression of revealed truth.

Potential Dangers

While it is true that Evangelicals have much in common with Roman Catholics, there are two dangers in considering Evangelical relationships with them. The first is to assert that all Roman Catholics are lost because of an implied faith in the historical episcopacy and the pope or faith in the institutional church and the Virgin Mary. Many, we believe, are saved in spite of the errors taught in that church, and this because of the measure of truth taught there and because of the wider dissemination of the Scriptures among Roman Catholics.

The second danger is to consider practicing Roman Catholics as being already regenerate because of their faithfulness to the church. This position was implied when the Consultation on World Evangelization at Pattaya, Thailand, in 1980 directed one of its strategies toward "The Christian Witness to Nominal Christians Among Roman Catholics." The great responsibility given by the Scriptures is to proclaim the biblical gospel to all, practicing Christians or non-Christians, so that each may have an opportunity to personally receive Jesus Christ by faith, trust Him as Savior and serve Him as Lord. Contrariwise, in the Roman Catholic Church, its ecclesiastical hierarchy and sacraments are seen as salvific. Most of the biblical issues of the Protestant Reformation are with us today and remind us that a common witness and work with the Roman Catholic Church can only confuse those seekers in that church and blunt the evangelistic efforts of Evangelicals.

The Lima 1982 document of the WCC entitled *Baptism, Eucharist and Ministry*[3] adds to the confusion. Theologians from Roman Catholic to Eastern Orthodox, from Methodists to Baptists, cooperated in a restatement of these teachings that may well bring Evangelicals into a greater worldwide theological crisis than the

---

[3] Faith and Order Paper 111 (Geneva: WCC, 1982).

fundamentalist-modernist confrontations of the early third part of this century. Evangelical unity will be challenged and threatened by this development as well.

Growing Tensions Among Evangelicals

A common theology, missions and evangelism are the dynamics and forces that give Evangelicalism a measure of unity and a united front to the world of religion and politics today. During the first half of this century Evangelical unity was anchored in a common rejection of and a reaction to liberalism and modernism. However, some problems that surfaced in the 1960s and blossomed in the 1970s have been increasingly disruptive in the 1980s.

One relates to the battle for the inspiration of the Scriptures and, ultimately, the authority of the Bible. This issue is not a dead one. It is like a Trojan horse in its conquest of Evangelical evangelism. Confidence in proclaiming "the Word" and in the promises of God assuring the believer of salvation is threatened. Furthermore, errancy leads to a far greater flexibility in the interpretation of the Scriptures and to an unwarranted contextualization of the message which then becomes "another gospel." This has already happened in some cases. For some, at least, the Bible seems to have lost its own inherent power and that of the Holy Spirit to convict, regenerate and convert.

The mission of the church is another point of contention. Historically, evangelism has been regarded as most basic. This was clearly affirmed in the International Congress on World Evangelization at Lausanne in 1974. Still, there were some present who felt that evangelism and social responsibility both deserved mission status, a view which was reflected in a minority report. Since Lausanne advocates of the minority position have become more vocal, it is difficult to forget that a similar stance of the WCC at its organization led to the demise of evangelism in the next generation.[4]

---

[4] An overall treatment of this historic position can be found in Harvey T. Hoekstra, *The World Council of Churches and the Demise of Evangelism* (Wheaton: Tyndale House, 1979); and Arthur P. Johnston, *World Evangelism and the Word of God* (Minneapolis: Bethany, 1974).

During the 1970s Evangelicals also began to speak of holistic, incarnational, or lordship evangelism. Some said that proclamation evangelism by itself was not evangelism at all unless it was "authenticated" by good works, concern for the whole man, social service, a kingdom life-style or work toward the transformation of a capitalistic economic structure to that of a socialistic system. Somehow they forgot the convicting power of the Scriptures and prayer, they forgot the authenticating power of the Holy Spirit, they forgot that no Christian or church can incarnate Christ, they forgot how the Wesley revivals and prayer influenced a degenerate English society and they forgot how evangelistic missions had uplifted communities and changed cultures and society on every continent where the gospel found a place in the hearts of people. Proponents of this new view also forgot that the Lord Himself promised to build His church and that the kingdom reign is in the hearts of believers until the King returns to rule and to transform a rebellious and sinful world now under the power of the evil one (1 John 5:19). The needs of individuals, of the church, and of the world have always been understood as a Christian duty or responsibility (Galatians 6:10).

Fermenting Problems

These issues within Evangelicalism proved to be not only controversial, but explosive. They brought a serious confrontation between representatives of these two groups at the first meeting of the Lausanne Committee for World Evangelization (LCWE) at Mexico City.[5] A further problem erupted at the Pattaya, Thailand, Consultation on World Evangelism (COWE) in 1980. Prior to COWE, Waldron Scott, then the WEF general secretary, invited Roman Catholic observers to the WEF's international meeting in England. These invitations were unacceptable to many, and it brought about the threat of resignation of the Spanish and the Italian Evangelical Alliances from the WEF. Scott's report to COWE of the WCC's

---

[5] See Arthur P. Johnston, *The Battle for World Evangelism* (Wheaton: Tyndale House, 1978), pp. 341–350.

Melbourne Meeting of the Division of World Mission and Evangelism, held a short time before Pattaya, seemed so positive on ecumenical kingdom theology that the WEF's future was perceived as
seriously compromised.

The kingdom issue surfaced again at the 1982 Grand Rapids,
Michigan, Consultation on the Relationship between Evangelism
and Social Responsibility, sponsored jointly by the WEF and the
LCWE. Ostensibly its purpose was to clarify ambiguous positions in
the Lausanne Covenant regarding the priority of evangelism. I was
shocked to hear a leading member of the WEF Theology Commission support the idea that the kingdom of God could be present on
earth now even where the gospel had never been preached! In other
words, the kingdom may be present in a place or culture where
there has been social, political, racial and economic justice established. And the kingdom can "come," it is proposed, by the transformation of society without the reign of Christ in regenerate hearts.
Premillenialism is especially rejected because of its pessimistic out-
look for the present world and its preoccupation with world evangelization.

Without denigrating the good work of the Theological Commission, we are obliged to ask if the goal of the church in mission is
world Christianization, world transformation or world evangelization. Is the church to be gathered in this age before Christ's return,
or is the kingdom on earth the primary objective of the cross and
the concern of the church? It is not surprising that a recently published journal is called *Transformation,* for the goal of mission has
changed from evangelism and church growth to societal transformation.

The tempo of this Evangelical dichotomy increased in Track III
of the "I Will Build My Church" Conference held at Wheaton and
also convened by the World Evangelical Fellowship. Track I, the
consultation on "The Church in the Local Setting," and Track II,
"The Church in New Frontiers for Missions" contributed to the
ongoing concern for world evangelization. However, Track III,
"The Church in Response to Human Need," introduced an entirely
new "Evangelical" theology of the kingdom. It is a synthesis between the non-Evangelical theology of the WCC in the 1960s and

that of historical Evangelicalism. In effect, societal transformation is presented as the kingdom goal of evangelism.[6]

Growing out of the meetings since Lausanne was the phrase "the priority of evangelism" in reference to the mission of the church. Whether intended or not, it implies that there are a number of other missions of the church. The effect is that social action is raised from the status of Christian duty or responsibility to become a mission of the church. In these last years "salvation" is no longer understood in terms of individual deliverance from sin's penalty and power, but in reference to sociopolitical deliverance from times of social, economic, racial and political oppression. In this church age, between the Ascension and the Second Coming, the kingdom is not necessarily in the heart of the believer or in the church but also upon the earth now. Exponents of Wheaton 1983 Track III adopted this kingdom position in their rightful concern for human needs. They declared the kingdom to be "both present and future, both societal and individual, both physical and spiritual." The kingdom, like a mustard seed, both judges and transforms the present age. God's purpose, they said, is to bless the nations, and so "the church is called to exist for the sake of its Lord and for the sake of humankind."[7] That is, world societies not only can be transformed now but they will be transformed as the church fulfills its mandate. God's saving activity in Christ, it is said, extends to all creation, and yet the world awaits the full and final consummation. The church exists for the societal welfare of the world and, thereby, it is participating in the extension and the expansion of the kingdom in this world. The church is a penultimate means and not a divinely ordained end in itself.

Unanswered Questions

This new gospel raises some serious questions concerning the "transformableness" of sinful man before the return of Christ. One wonders what this transformation theology has to say about the

---

[6] "The Church in Response to Human Need," July 1 (1983), pp. 7, 8.
[7] Ibid., p. 11.

lostness of man and eternal conscious punishment. In what sense is Satan the ruler of this present world? Are "principalities and powers" societal evils that need to be "exorcised" or are they demon personalities? What place does the church of born-again believers have in the eternal plan of God and how important is evangelism and the church in this age if it is God's penultimate goal to transform, in a measure, all societies of humankind? Is evangelism only one aspect of Christ's salvific work and thereby a means to the ultimate end of a transformed kingdom society? A similar position was adopted by the WCC in their Melbourne 1980 meeting entitled "Your Kingdom Come," but most Evangelicals at COWE 1980 rejected the presuppositions and content of this report as a sub-Evangelical, liberation theme. The Bible simply does not teach an optimistic view of human history in this age, though evangelism and the resultant churches do transform individual lives, families, communities and nations by the blessings of a gracious God.

Evangelicalism is being stretched beyond the bonds of the Scriptures by nonbiblical appeals from the WCC, from Roman Catholicism and from the "Evangelical" transformationists. The boundaries can snap. Unity is again being sought by some Evangelicals who are willing to compromise doctrine.

The drift to the left generally begins with a less-than-inerrant view of the Scriptures. Into this vacuum of authority steps the institutional churches leaning upon their historic tradition. The authority of the church or churches replaces the authority of Scripture. Evangelism and the growth of the church lose their importance. Emphasis then drifts to the physical needs of man in contrast to the eternal punishment awaiting the unregenerate. Evangelism is first seen as a primary responsibility; then as an equal to social service, political action or transformation; then as a means to the societal goals of God and; finally, as irrelevant.

Questions for Thought

1. How is the unity given to those in Christ manifested in the world? (John 13:34–35.)

2. What are those essential teachings of the Scriptures around which believers are united? (Note 1 Corinthians 15:1–4.)

3. When is disunity required by the Scriptures? (Note Galatians 1:6–10; Romans 16:17.)

4. What influence does unity have upon effective evangelism?

5. What influence does disunity within a church have upon evangelism?

6. At what point can a nonbiblical unity stifle and even extinguish evangelism? (Note 2 John 4–10; Jude 3–23.)

7. Can the evident growth of Evangelical evangelism in many places of the world be hindered by developing unbiblical relationships that distort the biblical message?

3

Biblical Integrity and Revival

Wayne A. Detzler

Wayne Detzler is an Assistant Professor of Mission in the School of World Mission and Evangelism at Trinity Evangelical Divinity School. He received both a B.A. in history and an M.A. in church history from Wheaton College and went on to earn a Ph.D. in church history from Manchester University in England.

Before coming to Trinity in September, 1983, Dr. Detzler served as the Associate European Director of Greater Europe Mission. Later he became pastor of Kensington Baptist Church in Bristol, England. He has also served on the faculty of Trinity College in Bristol, England; Moorlands Bible College in Sopley, England; and the German Bible Institute in Seeheim, Germany.

An experienced author, Dr. Detzler has written several books, including *The Changing Church in Europe,* and four books in the *Living Words* series on Ephesians, 1 Peter, 1 Corinthians and Philippians. His most recent release is *New Testament Words in Today's Language.* He is also a contributor to many periodicals. When living in England he regularly spoke over the BBC network.

Spiritual Vitality and the Scriptures

God intends for His people to abound in fullness of life and be fruitful through His Spirit. Where this is not experienced, we need revival, which means simply to come alive to the provisions of grace promised in His Word.

Revival goes hand in hand with belief in the Bible. Persons alive to the Spirit are convinced that the God who inspired the Scriptures also guarantees their accuracy. Not only is the authority of the Scriptures accepted; it is also obeyed, which, in turn, assures the perpetuation of the gospel.

Everything hinges on faithfulness to the Word. The Scriptures warn that pedantic, petty legalism is hypocritical. Only as Christians live by God's truth do they experience divine blessing. When they allow the Holy Spirit to "integrate" the Bible into their behavior, they are able to make an impact upon the world powerfully with their witness. As a result people are saved, and the church accomplishes the purpose for which she was born: the evangelization of the lost.

To develop this principle of biblical integrity, let us consider it from two opposing standpoints. First, we will see what happens when the church quenches the Holy Spirit and denies the authority of the Scriptures. Second, we shall survey situations in which the Holy Spirit empowers God's people to believe and preach the Word of God. This chapter is a study in contrasts.

Tragedy of Bible Neglect

The danger of rejecting the Scriptures is seen in the history of Israel. One example occurred prior to the rise of King Josiah in Judah. Although the Northern Kingdom of Israel had been swept away by Assyria, the Southern Kingdom continued in its idolatrous ways. Temple worship had long since been discarded, and all manner of evil had replaced faithfulness to Jehovah. Instead of purity, prostitution was practiced in the very temple precincts. Instead of worshiping the invisible God Jehovah, idols were placed before the people and commended by successive evil rulers. Instead of offering sacrifices to Jehovah, the people of Judah offered their babies to the god Moloch. They laid infants on the red-hot arms of Moloch's statue until life was seared out of their little bodies.

The reason for these perversions was ignorance of the Scriptures. The Law of God was neither read nor practiced by the people of Judah. Prophets who preached the Word of God were imprisoned and rejected, as can be seen in the stories of Jeremiah and Isaiah. The kings of Judah had turned their backs on Jehovah and embraced the false gods of other nations. The prophet Amos called this a "famine for the Word of God" (*see* Amos 8:11).

Just as ignorance of the Scriptures plunged Israel into sin, so it also made the Middle Ages of Europe the Dark Ages. When William Tyndale started to translate the Bible into English, there was a vast and general ignorance of the Scriptures. The medieval church had banned laymen from reading the Bible. Any attempt to make the Bible available to the common people was rigorously rejected by the religious authorities. At the Council of Constance (1415) John Huss was burned for bringing the Bible to the people. The same sessions ordered the exhumation of John Wycliffe's bones, so that they could be burned. He too had translated the Bible into the language of the people, in his case, English. Church authorities threatened to excommunicate anyone who would translate the Bible into the vernacular. As a result of these strong-arm tactics the Bible was banished from the homes of the people, and the Holy Spirit was excluded from the councils of the church.[1]

In the same way, the Enlightenment era of the late eighteenth century eclipsed the light of the Scriptures. Parading under the flag of Deism, many articulate and urbane thinkers set about to undercut the authority of the Scriptures. One of these was Jean-Jacques Rousseau (1712–1778). He asserted that human reason is the ultimate source of truth. As a Deist, he insisted that God had created people and given them the intelligence to run the world. Because human beings are endowed by their Creator with intelligence, he contended, God no longer concerns Himself with the operation of the world. By the same token, human intelligence is believed to be far more reliable than the Scriptures. Thus reason is set up as judge over revelation. This view is called rationalism.[2]

---

[1] Philip Schaff, *A History of the Christian Church,* VII (New York: Charles Scribner's Sons, 1892–1926), p. 11.

[2] For a brief review of this position, see Karl Barth, *Protestant Theology from Rousseau to Ritschl* (New York: Simon and Schuster, 1969), pp. 86, 138, 167–8; and Tim Dowley, ed., *Eerdmans' Handbook to the History of Christianity* (Grand Rapids: William B. Eerdmans, 1977), p. 492.

Another advocate of this "rationalism" was Francois-Marie Arouet (1694–1778), alias Voltaire. He scoffed at the Scriptures, asserting that people were wise enough to reason out the solutions to life's problems. He also snidely suggested that the Bible would fade completely from sight within a few years of his death. Ironically, fifteen years after his demise, his home in Paris became a warehouse in which the British and Foreign Bible Society stored the Scriptures.

The Drift Today

There are many parallels to these dismal scenes in contemporary culture. Despite the estimated numerical strength of American Evangelical Christianity, spiritual malnutrition is gnawing away at its vital organs. For example, in September, 1983, the Christian Broadcasting Network commissioned a Gallup Poll of religious interest in America. Fifty-seven percent of the people polled (1029 in all), indicated that their spiritual sensitivity had increased over the previous five years. On the other hand, fewer than 12 percent felt that they were "deeply religious." Gallup concluded that: "Churches have not helped to bring the Bible" into the people's lives.[3]

Shortly before his death, the brilliant analyst of Evangelical Christianity, Francis Schaeffer, wrote *The Great Evangelical Disaster*. His conclusion was devastating in its directness: "Here is the great Evangelical disaster—the failure of the Evangelical world to stand for truth as truth ... the Evangelical church has accommodated to the world spirit of the age."[4]

Along the same lines Bruce Buursma, religion writer for the *Chicago Tribune*, publicized a study undertaken by the Wheaton-based American Resource Bureau. "Many born-again people want faith to be easy," he concluded. Evangelicals "are not interested in hearing about—much less experiencing—the suffering that following

---

[3] Beth Spring, "A Gallup Poll Finds a Rising Tide of Interest in Religion," *Christianity Today* (October 21, 1983), p. 41.

[4] Francis A. Schaeffer, *The Great Evangelical Disaster* (Westchester, IL: Crossways Books, 1984), p. 37.

Jesus may demand . . . or seeking God's will, or the material sacrifices that are expected of those who are devoted" to Christ.[5]

There seem to be two main reasons for this tragic account. First,
many so-called Evangelicals have begun to hedge on the issue of
biblical inerrancy. No longer sure that the Bible is really the Word
of God, they do not conform to its teachings about the inviolability
of marriage, the importance of honesty in business, or the clear line
of separation between believers and the world. In fact, during the
past three decades many of these scriptural teachings have been
relegated to a by-gone age.

A second parallel problem is insensitivity to the Holy Spirit. Sel-
dom is there any sense of repentance among Christians. To many
the cultivation of a glowing self-image has replaced the development of the image of Christ in us. Talk about sanctification by the
Holy Spirit is carefully filed away as fanaticism.

As a result of these twin troubles, the witness of many Evangelical Christians lacks credibility. The world sees no clear difference
between itself and the church. In such an environment evangelism
is easily eclipsed by social action or religious entertainment.

The President of the Southern Baptist Convention, Dr. Charles
Stanley, responded to a newspaper interview with this assessment of
American religion at the end of 1984:

> Our challenge is to bring people into line with God's truth
> rather than man's fashion. What we have now is not a new
> morality, just the old morality. Over the years, there has
> been a tremendous erosion of the authority of the Word of
> God. The ideas of men have crept in. Unless the Bible re-
> mains inerrant in the eyes of the church, then the truth
> and effectiveness of Christianity is neutered and no longer
> provides the force and the life that is necessary.[6]

So here we see the negative illustration of our principle. When
the Scriptures are ignored or devalued as being merely human
words, the Holy Spirit is quenched. Christians remain cold and

---

[5] *Chicago Tribune* (October 6, 1984).
[6] *USA Today* (December 24, 1984).

dead, despite numerical strength and material wealth. Any attempt to proclaim the gospel is muted by the misery of this meaningless religion. The only hope is spiritual revival.

Seen Throughout History

Revival comes when the Holy Spirit ignites the Word of God and burns it into the hearts and minds of God's people. This principle was illustrated in the life of King Josiah. When he came to the throne, Judah was dead, as we have seen. He sought out the Law and had it read publicly (2 Kings 22:8–13; 23:1–3). The result was a dramatic awakening. The idols were removed from Jehovah's temple and incinerated (2 Kings 23:4–6). Homosexual prostitutes were likewise banished (2 Kings 23:7). False prophets were rejected. Idolatrous chapels were razed. Between the coronation of Josiah (640 B.C.) and his untimely death in 609 B.C., revival restored the spiritual state of Israel. All of this was the result of reading and heeding the Law of God.

The same attention to the Scriptures produced the Reformation of the sixteenth century. Although they were killed for their commitment to the Scriptures, Tyndale, Wycliffe and Huss had a worthy successor in Martin Luther. He translated the Bible into German and declared that all Christians are priests with the privilege of reading and understanding the Scriptures. It is easy to understand the assessment of Philip Schaff, the great German-American historian, who concluded that, "a most important part of the Reformation was the vernacular translation of the Bible."[7]

Not only did Martin Luther "unleash the lion of Scripture," but Calvin also followed this pattern. He took up the French Bible as translated by Jacques d'Etaples Lefevre and taught it to the people of Geneva. In his *Institutes of the Christian Religion,* John Calvin argued that every Christian controlled by the Holy Spirit is capable of interpreting the Scriptures. To aid the individual Calvin carefully taught through the Scriptures, verse by verse. Every day he held evangelistic Bible studies in the church at Geneva.

---

[7] Schaff, *A History of the Christian Church,* VIII, p. 33.

As Luther let the light of the Scriptures into Germany, and Calvin taught the Bible in Geneva, so the English Reformation revolved around the Bible. Although Tyndale and Wycliffe had met resistance, Henry VIII commissioned a new edition of Tyndale's Testament in 1525 and Miles Coverdale's Bible in 1535. He, too, insisted on the universal distribution of the Scriptures.[8]

The direction of the Scriptures issued in a reformation of the church throughout Europe. As a result, justification by faith was preached, and people were converted to Christ. "Every Christian could henceforth go to the fountainhead of inspiration and sit at the feet of the Divine Teacher, without priestly permission or intervention."[9]

Unfortunately, in the century following the Reformation, the church cooled off as dead orthodoxy replaced real spiritual life. It took the Pietist and, later, the Wesleyan revivals to breathe new life into the dry bones. Both of these movements had their roots in the holy Scriptures. John Wesley represented it well when he declared: "I want to know the way to heaven. God has written it down in a book. O give me that book! At any price, give me the book of God."[10] For him the inerrancy of the Scriptures was a corollary to God's integrity. "If there be any mistake in the Bible," he said, "then there may as well be a thousand. If there is one falsehood in that book, then it certainly did not come as the truth from God."[11]

Wesley's sometime colleague, George Whitefield, believed the Bible with the same intensity of conviction. Wherever he went, on both sides of the Atlantic, he preached the Word of the Lord. Following the same pattern, there sprang up in the American colonies a "Great Awakening" under the ministry of the Tennents, Jonathan Edwards, and Theodore Frelinghuysen. In every case their preaching was based upon, built by, and bounded by the book of God.

The grandson of Jonathan Edwards was Timothy Dwight, who became President of Yale College in 1795. At the time Dwight as-

---

[8] Tim Dowley, ed., *Eerdmans' Handbook to the History of Christianity* (Grand Rapids: Eerdmans, 1974), p. 368.
[9] Schaff, *A History of the Christian Church,* VII, p. 11.
[10] Quoted by Kenneth S. Kantzer, "Mission—and the Church's Authority," *The Church's Worldwide Mission* (Waco: Word Books, 1966), p. 30.
[11] John Wesley, *The Journal of the Rev. John Wesley,* Nehemiah Curnock, ed., VI (London: Robert Culley, 1909), p. 117.

sumed his office, only a handful of students on campus professed faith in Christ. In order to rectify this situation, the President preached in chapel a series of sermons with the title: "Is the Bible the Word of God?"[12] Like his grandfather, Dwight believed in the inerrancy of the Bible, and the Holy Spirit enabled him to preach it with power. More than one-third of the skeptical students were converted, and a great revival swept through the college.

During the nineteenth century, the Second Evangelical Awakening moved across Europe, Britain, and the United States. In Europe men such as Robert Haldane, Hans Nielsen Hauge, and the Krummacher brothers preached the Word under the inspiration of the Holy Spirit. The result was a revival which embraced much of central and northern Europe. In America the same pattern emerged through the Methodist circuit riders and Baptist frontier preachers. The impact of the awakening continued for decades. Reflecting on this era, a perceptive Christian observed: "Such remarkable revivals of religion afford strong evidences that the Scriptures are from God, since the truths contained in them are attended with such divine power in awakening, reforming, and renewing sinners."[13]

Still Time Today

Revival through the Holy Spirit anointed preaching of the Scriptures is not just a phenomenon of history. During the past thirty-five years Billy Graham has proven the same point in a powerful way. Beginning with the Los Angeles crusade of 1949, he has preached the gospel simply, punctuating his message with the phrase, "the Bible says."

There was a time in his early preaching, though, when Billy Graham was strongly tempted to doubt the truth of the Scriptures. Knowing that the conflict must be resolved, he went out into an isolated place and wrestled this question through with God. In

---

[12] Timothy Dwight, *Theology Explained and Defended in a Series of Sermons by Timothy Dwight,* Stevens Dwight, ed. (Edinburgh, 1831), pp. xxiii–xxiv.
[13] Bennett Taylor, *New England Revivals,* reprint ed. (Wheaton: Richard Owen Roberts, 1980), p. 207.

prayer he received the assurance that the Bible is true, and that he could preach it as the Word of God.[14] From that point onward, his preaching has exemplified the two pillars of biblical integrity: scriptural authority and Spirit anointing.

There has been an undeniable link between faithfulness to the Bible and revival, from the time of Moses until this present day. Where there is an implicit and explicit confidence in the Scriptures, the Holy Spirit descends in power on that congregation of worshipers. The result is a credible witness to the believer, and evangelism flourishes. This is the prerogative of every generation and every individual Christian. How tragic when one becomes content with a formal faith which is devoid of life!

Revival has been necessary in every generation. The unusual popularity of Evangelical Christianity in our time tends to mask that need with a superficial gloss of success. However, underneath this facade the need still persists. The prevailing state of the church seems woefully inadequate to stem the tide of iniquity in our day. It is time for judgment to begin at the house of God. I am reminded of a sign put up in a churchyard: "This church will either have a revival or a funeral." That banner could well be flown over contemporary Christianity.

Conditions for Revival

The biblical prerequisites for revival are frequently repeated in the Old and New Testaments. They are best summarized in 2 Chronicles 7:14: "If my people, who are called by my name, will humble themselves and pray and seek my face and turn from their wicked ways, then will I hear from heaven and will forgive their sin and will heal their land" (NIV). There are four elemental principles in this verse: relationship, repentance, restoration, and regeneration.

First, the whole verse has a relationship as its premise. This challenge is not directed to the pagans who follow their idols. It is aimed

---

[14] John Pollock, *Billy Graham: The Authorized Biography* (London: Hodder and Stoughton, 1966), pp. 78–79.

at the people of Israel. Revival always begins with the house of God.

The Reformation arose not in a land devoid of Christian consciousness, but rather in the midst of a very austere Augustinian monastery. It was there that Martin Luther discovered his spiritual need and entered upon a search which ultimately led him to justification by faith. The Holy Spirit applied the Word of God to the heart of a desperate seeker.

When Wesley arrived in the American colonies, he was a missionary. At Oxford he had helped to establish the Holy Club. His faithfulness to the study of the Scriptures had earned him the derisory title of "Methodist," because of the methodical nature of his study. It was this sincere seeker of truth, a man who served God wholeheartedly, that God finally saved at Aldersgate.

Many years ago I was preaching in a small village in Germany. During our two weeks there we had seen a rather remarkable ingathering of souls. I was puzzled until one day we visited an old farmhouse. There I met a grandmother who had prayed sixty or seventy years for revival. Again, revival began in the heart of a sincere believer.

Revival is built upon a relationship. Unless there is some spiritual relationship, revival will not come. God responds to the sincere prayer of His people, no matter how faintly their faith flickers.

Second, revival involves repentance. There must be a turning from sin. The Chronicles verse speaks of humbling oneself, turning from sin, and seeking God's face. These are all part of biblical repentance. When this repentance is present, God will always respond with a reviving touch.

W. P. Nicholson was conducting a revival crusade in Northern Ireland. One day he stopped to see a shopkeeper and invited him to attend the meetings. "I shall never come to your meetings," the shopkeeper responded.

"Why are you so adamant?" asked the preacher.

"Well, many people in this town owe me money," responded the businessman. Then he added, "Most of my debtors claim to be Christians and attend your meetings."

That night Nicholson said: "I invited a shopkeeper to attend the meetings, but he refused because you owe him money. Unless you pay your debts, I shall read your names out publicly." Soon almost every shopkeeper in town had his bad debts cleared. Revival came.

Revival always rides on the carriage of repentance. When the revival broke out in Wales in 1904, many factories had to open whole departments to receive back stolen tools. Repentance involved returning stolen goods. In the same revival many of the miners quit swearing, and the pit ponies which pulled the mine trains came to a standstill, because they could not understand the commands of their revived drivers. (This story was confirmed to me by none other than a pit pony driver from Wales.)

Repentance is not simply sorrow for wrongs done. It is far more a turning from sin, as the Chronicles verse says. When this sincere, active repentance occurs, God unleashes revival. Too often we confess "nice, socially acceptable" sins. There needs to be a complete honesty with God if we would have revival.

Third, revival involves restoration of the backslidden believer. In the same Welsh revival of 1904 a village lass went one evening to the nearby town. For weeks she had been under the burden of conviction; now she went to hear Evan Roberts, the great revival personality. Late that night she returned to the village. As she proceeded through the village street, she paused and knocked at each door. When an answer came she said simply: "He's lifted the burden, He's lifted the burden!" God had restored the joy of her salvation. Revival always produces restoration of wounded faith.

The same is true on a churchwide scale. Some years ago the Rev. Malcolm Widdecombe was appointed to a dying parish in the center of Bristol, England. Under his ministry a great revival fell upon that struggling parish. Hardly a Sunday passed without conversions. The needy people of Bristol were reached with the gospel message. A church which had been targeted by the bishop for closure was restored and revived. The result is a witness which continues still.

An identical experience is recounted from the city of York, England. The late David Weston was appointed by the Archbishop of York to St. Michael-le-Bellfrey. There he preached the Word with power. Instead of closing the church, it was revived and blessing streamed from that little parish throughout Britain.

Fourth and finally, revival issues in the conversion of the lost. Evangelism and revival are not to be confused, but they are also not to be separated. They go hand in hand. When the Holy Spirit ignites the Word of God, Christians come alive, and so do sinners.

This can be observed throughout history. For example, surveying the Second Evangelical Awakening in America, Professor Timothy Smith sketched the scope of conversions. He found that the Methodist Church in America grew from 1.57 million members in 1855 to 2.01 million members a decade later. Over the same period the Baptists increased from 1.1 million to 1.35 million. The Presbyterian Church, although smaller than Methodists and Baptists, grew from 495,715 to 616,617.[15]

Writing about the same awakening, Edwin Orr concentrated on the 1857 prayer revival. It began with six praying people. Soon their number grew to 10,000. As a result at least 2 million were converted.[16] When God's people are filled with the Holy Spirit, they invariably reach out to the unconverted and draw them into the rejuvenated fellowship.

The Issue Before the Church

Revival is a closely woven spiritual tapestry. It has the inerrant Scriptures as its warp and the living, powerful Holy Spirit as its woof. The colors are woven in by God's people who repent and are restored. New threads are always being added as sinners are saved. The picture on this tapestry is none other than the image of the Lord Jesus Christ.

O that we could see more of this image today! Never before have there been so many strong seminaries and thriving Evangelical churches. Even political personalities take the Evangelicals into account. Their public influence has never been greater. However, our spiritual strength seems to be sapped. We may claim to believe the Bible, but the power of its witness in our lives is lacking. Until biblical knowledge is galvanized with action, our nation will remain unreached. Any discussion of evangelism must face this issue.

---

[15] Timothy L. Smith, *Revivalism and Social Reform in Mid-Nineteenth Century America* (Nashville: Abingdon Press, 1957), pp. 19–20.

[16] J. Edwin Orr, *The Second Evangelical Awakening* (London: Marshall, Morgan, and Scott, 1978), p. 248.

Questions for Thought

1. What consequences resulted when Israel ceased to obey the Law of God?

2. Why did the pre-Reformation church regard the Scriptures as being so dangerous?

3. If Evangelicals claim they are faithful to the Bible, why is there such a gap between this claim and the practice of Christianity?

4. What relationship existed between the revivals under Wesley and Jonathan Edwards and their commitments to the Scriptures?

5. Using the evangelism of Billy Graham as an illustration, what connection is seen between a biblical commitment and evangelistic fruitfulness?

6. What steps should be taken to bring contemporary belief and behavior into line with the Bible?

4

The Cry for Justice and Liberation

William D. Taylor

William D. Taylor is Associate Professor of Latin American Missions and Cross-Cultural Christian Education in the School of World Mission and Evangelism at Trinity Evangelical Divinity School. Previously he was on the faculty of the Central American Theological Seminary in Guatemala, where he served as Chairman of the Department of Ministry. He has also taught at the Latin American Mission Biblical Seminary in Costa Rica, and Dallas Theological Seminary.

He is a graduate of Moody Bible Institute, North Texas State University, Dallas Theological Seminary, and received the Ph.D. in sociology and anthropology of education and Latin American Studies at the University of Texas.

The son of missionary parents, Dr. Taylor has lived for nearly three decades in Central America, where he has served with CAM International. In addition to teaching, he has worked with various youth ministries, and planted a church in Guatemala City, which is now a thriving congregation.

His publications include *La Pirámide del Amor, La Familea Autenticamente Cristiana* and *Latin America: A Personal Perspective.* He has also written a series of applied Bible studies, and numerous articles for magazines.

Facing the Reality

The cry for social justice and liberation is heard around the world. It may be a result of human violence—personal or structured into the society—or it may result from acts of nature which produce famine and other devastations. Making the condition increasingly

59

acute is the exploding population, particularly in the two-thirds world. According to statistics from the Population Reference Bureau, the "more developed" nations of the world as of mid-1984 had a population of 1,166,000,000 growing at an annual rate of 0.6 percent per year. The "less developed" nations already had a mid-1984 population of 3,596,000,000, *but* they were growing at a rate of 2.1 percent per year.[1] This means that while the "more developed" will double within a distant 112 years, the "less developed" will double within a dramatic thirty-three years. And much of the obvious social injustice and yearning for liberation that we read about is located in the latter group of nations. This in no way minimizes the cry for social justice and liberation within the European Marxist nations, about which too few Evangelicals and secular prophets on the topic are speaking!

So why a chapter on this topic in this book on evangelism? At the outset let us establish the absolute priority of the eternal saving gospel of Jesus Christ. No human social justice and liberation will solve the fundamental spiritual separation between God and man. So why in this book? In the first place because it is a biblical issue which now must be dealt with seriously. The Lausanne Covenant is succinct: "We affirm that God is both the Creator and the Judge of all men. We therefore should share His concern for justice and reconciliation throughout human society and for the liberation of men from every kind of oppression."[2]

Second, this theme touches the very heart of the church's mission and its commission to disciple the nations, "teaching them to observe all things I have commanded." Biblical evangelism is not a head/soul-hunting crusade; rather, it centers in human lives, seeing them transformed by the saving knowledge of Christ and integrated into authentic local churches. But man must live by both breads—the primary Word of God bread and the materially nourishing breads as crucial for human sustenance.

A third reason for including this essay is that I would like to represent some of the voices from the two-thirds world, where

---

[1] Population Reference Bureau, Inc., 2213 M Street, N.W., Washington, D.C. The statistics come from the 1984 World Population Data Sheet.
[2] The Lausanne Covenant, in *Let the Earth Hear His Voice* (Minneapolis: World Wide Publications, 1975), p. 4.

Evangelicals with full trust in the nature and authority of the Scriptures are allowing the Word to ask them new questions and permit new answers. At the same time these brothers and sisters in Christ are asking the Word new questions and seeking for new answers that respond to their concrete human condition. In a sense this chapter is a request for mutual understanding and trust between biblical students in our interdependent, worldwide Evangelical community.

Many Voices Heard

As we acknowledge the reality of the issue, we also realize that the panoply of individuals who attempt to speak on the issue today must be evaluated with great care. This central topic is a battle cry of Marxism and certain strands of socialism, particularly those surging from within the two-thirds world. Social justice and liberation themes are central in the writings of Roman Catholics and Protestants who advocate liberation theologies.[3]

There is also a growing number of articulate Evangelicals from the Anglo-Saxon nations as well as Latin America, Asia and Africa who are speaking with force on the topic. They will offer a wide spectrum of opinions, from polemicists Jim Wallis to Franky Schaeffer; from Emilio Antonio Núñez of Central America, who writes on liberation theology from the perspective of a Latin American Evangelical, to Ronald Nash, who speaks on the same topic but from the limited lens of North American understanding; from the practical "this is how we are doing it" approach of John Perkins to "these are some ways to do it" approach by Miriam Adeney and Richard Cizik; from Anglo Tom Sine to Indian Vinay Samuel in their attempts to respond to human need from a Christian perspective.[4]

---

[3] Two representatives: the Argentine Methodist Jose Miquez Bonino, *Doing Theology in a Revolutionary Situation* (Philadelphia: Fortress Press, 1975) and the Peruvian Catholic "Systematizer," Gustavo Gutiérrez, *A Theology of Liberation* (Maryknoll, N.Y.: Orbis Books, 1973).

[4] Cf. Jim Wallis, *The Call to Conversion: Recovering the Gospel for These Times* (San Francisco: Harper and Row, 1981); Franky Schaeffer, *Bad News for*

As we demonstrate our concern for social justice and liberation today we must be keenly aware that the secular and truly nonbiblical ideologies and voices will try to set the agenda for the church. We must not allow this to occur, lest we lose sight of our scriptural priorities. One specific case in point is liberation theology (or, more correctly, the liberation theologies), "which in its more radical forms filters the Christian message through a Marxist-influenced social analysis of the class struggle."[5] While we understand the structural flaws of liberation theology—its substitution of political ideology for biblical authority, particularly Marxist, with the logical consequences—we must appreciate *why* it emerges on the scene. We must listen to Gutiérrez and evaluate his criticism of traditional theology,[6] as well as his own surrogate with its inherently flawed hermeneutic. Evangelicals such as Padilla and Núñez have interacted, from within their Latin American world with liberationist reflections of the Scriptures, and have affirmed the centrality of the contextualized Word of God, their supracultural authority.[7]

Defining Our Concepts

Latin Americans have a sardonic proverb: "In this traitorous world there is no truth nor lie; it all depends on the lens to which we put the eye." The saying applies to our definitions of terms, for

Modern Man: An Agenda for Christian Action (Westchester, IL: Crossway Books, 1984); Emilio Antonio Núñez, (Chicago: Moody Press, 1985); Ronald H. Nash, ed. *Liberation Theology* (Milford, MI: Mott Media, 1984); John Perkins, *A Quiet Revolution: The Christian Response to Human Need. . . . A Strategy for Today* (Waco: Word Books, 1976); Miriam Adeney, *God's Foreign Policy: Practical Ways to Help the World's Poor* (Grand Rapids: Eerdmans, 1984); Richard Cizik, ed. *The High Cost of Indifference: Can Christians Afford Not to Act?* (Ventura, CA: Regal Books, 1984); Tom Sine, ed. *The Church in Response to Human Need* (Monrovia, CA: MARC, 1983); Vinay Samuel and Chris Sugden, eds. *Evangelism and the Poor: a Third World Study Guide* (Oxford, England: Oxford Centre for Mission Studies, 1982).
[5] *Time* (February 18, 1985), p. 34.
[6] Gustavo Gutiérrez, *A Theology of Liberation,* Chapter 1.
[7] C. Rene Padilla, "The Theology of Liberation," Third International Conference of Institutions for Christian Higher Education, Dordt College, Sioux City, Iowa, August 13–20, 1981, unpublished ms. Núñez cited above.

words mean what we want them to mean. When Harold Lindsell speaks of social justice and property rights he speaks from his own lens perspective, but when Roman Catholic historian Dussel speaks on the topic, his total perspective is radically different.[8]

A dictionary will offer basic, stipulative definitions which give a starting point for language understanding. However, it is when words are put together, interpreted and incarnated that the true significance takes place. *Social* speaks "of or relating to human society, the interaction of the individual and the group, or the welfare of human beings as members of a society." *Justice* is defined as "the maintenance or administration of what is just especially by the impartial adjustment of conflicting claims or the assignment of merited rewards or punishments." It is also "the quality of being just, impartial, or fair." And *liberation* is conceived of as "the action of seeking equal rights and status."[9]

The dictionary gives us a point of departure, and we can then begin to integrate the terms, moving them from printed paper to dynamic human experience. But we cannot stop there, for as Christians we take our final authority from the Word of God. Unfortunately many Evangelical authors write on the topic of social justice and liberation but do not define their terms adequately, if at all. Packer is a good exception to this rule when he defines the term *liberty* while at the same time helping out on the term *justice*.

> The biblical idea of liberty [freedom] has as its background the thought of imprisonment or slavery. . . . When the Bible speaks of liberty, a prior bondage of incarceration is always implied. Liberty means the happy state of having been released from servitude for a life of enjoyment and satisfaction that was not possible before. The idea of liberty appears in Scripture in its ordinary secular applications . . . but it also receives a significant theologi-

---

[8] Harold Lindsell, *Free Enterprise: A Judeo-Christian Defense* (Wheaton, IL: Tyndale House Publications, Inc., 1982). Enrique Dussel, *A History of the Church in Latin America: Colonialism to Liberation* (Grand Rapids: Eerdmans Publishing Company, 1981). Lindsell's idealized economics contrast with Dussel's ideals for land reform in Latin America.

[9] *Webster's New Collegiate Dictionary* (Springfield, MA: G. & C. Merriam Co., Publishers, 1983).

cal development. This sprang from Israel's realization that such freedom from subjugation by foreigners as she enjoyed was God's gift to her. In the NT liberty becomes an important theological concept for describing salvation.[10]

How do we use the terms as Evangelicals? We are speaking of a broad category of concerns that have to do with the relationship between the eternal Word of God and His saving gospel and the fractured, unjust human condition in a broken world. We seek authentic equity between human beings, for true freedom from oppressions. Social justice within the context of North America seems to focus at present on the struggles against pornography, homosexual rights, abortion, euthanasia, and the nuclear arms race. The two-thirds world's struggles may include the above, but they go on to many other issues, such as the social responsibility of the Christian, wealth/poverty, human rights violations, housing shortages, unjust treatment of Indian peoples, constitution writing, violence, and personal/structural injustice. By the latter we refer to the institutionalization of legal and political systems, which by design are created to benefit traditional elites and nourish poverty and oppression. Social justice here is not a theoretical abstract. It is visceral. In the Anglo-Saxon countries these concerns are limited to working within the existing political system, with a heritage of democracy, but in other nations the political system is still being defined. This obviously injects vastly different categories of theological reflection and social action. I am utilizing the broadest categories expressed in this paragraph as my working definitions.

Understanding Our Use of the Bible

Again the lens to which we put our eye is crucial, and nobody is totally objective in his approach and response to the Bible. We all start from our own context and preunderstandings. Mott discusses

---

[10] J. I. Packer in "Justice," *The Illustrated Bible Dictionary,* Vol. 2 (Wheaton, IL: Tyndale House Publishers, 1980), pp. 839–841.

this in his study on biblical ethics and social change, and acknowledges the subjectivity factor.

> The interpretation of Scripture begins in the life experience of listening in faith as the Word of God is read and taught and of obedient conduct guided by this Word. Among the truths experienced in this way, the biblical message of justice creates a basic loyalty to the poor and weak and a commitment to their defense. Scripture is then interpreted in the light of this biblically formed understanding.

> But the interpreter of the social ethics of Scripture brings to the text not only a disposition shaped by his or her experience and background. The interpreter's own focus on social need has led to an increased interest in all that can be known about social and economic structures and ways of expressing and evaluating social norms.[11]

It is fascinating how many different interpretations can be given to the biblical teaching on social justice and liberation, all depending on the presuppositions. Whether it is Conn or Cone, Mott or Miranda, Sider or Schaeffer, Padilla or Pixley, all utilize the Bible with their particular concept of authority.[12] Our preunderstandings regarding the nature of the Scriptures affect our entire theology and praxis.

A Marxist starts from his interpretation of history, and it is a secular, horizontal, nonrevelational conception. Liberation theology

---

[11] Stephen Charles Mott, *Biblical Ethics and Social Change* (New York: Oxford University Press, 1982), p. vii.

[12] Cf. Harvie M. Conn, *Evangelism: Doing Justice and Preaching Grace* (Grand Rapids: Zondervan Publishing House, 1982); James Cone, a Black Liberation Theologian, writes in *God of the Oppressed* (New York: Seabury Press, 1975); Mott in *Biblical Ethics and Social Change;* Jose Porfirio Miranda in *Communism and the Bible* (Maryknoll: Orbis, 1982); Ronald J. Sider, *Rich Christians in an Age of Hunger* (Downers Grove, IL: Inter-Varsity Press, 1977); Schaeffer in *Bad News for Modern Man;* Padilla in his essay on liberation theology and as editor of *Misión,* an evangelical missiological journal in Spanish; Jorge Pixley in *Exodo: Una Lectura Evangélica y Popular* (Mexico: Casa Unida de Publicaciones, 1983).

proponents, not always Marxist oriented, start from the context of poverty and oppression. The defender of capitalism, whether in a democratic spirit or not, fundamentally starts from economics, although Lindsell strains hard to prove that capitalism/free enterprise is truly the biblical economic system.[13]

Yet others see no need for concern regarding biblical teaching on social justice and liberation. To them the mission of the church is exclusively a spiritual one of soul saving, with a truncated concept both of the church's mission and the implications of the gospel. Most of them simply ignore the topic, naively hoping it will go away. Then there are some vocal, and at times strident, voices on the Evangelical "left wing" who challenge many weaknesses of the church, but their ideological and political presuppositions have confused their perspective.[14]

What we need are more Evangelicals who are at the same time biblically literate and compassionate, and who with the highest view of the Scriptures will contextualize their theology in the lives of precious humans. Believers and nonbelievers live in the bitter reality of historical oppression and poverty, injustice and violence. They need and deserve a biblical evangelism which does justice and preaches grace.[15]

It is risky to suggest hermeneutical guidelines in this brief chapter, but there are fundamental issues to keep in mind as we utilize Scripture in this context.[16] To begin, we must seek for the original authorial intent and meaning. This is a prime norm because it es-

---

[13] Cf. Lindsell in work cited previously, and Catholic neoconservative Michael Novak, *The Spirit of Democratic Capitalism* (New York: Simon and Schuster Publications, 1982). Novak has one of the best-documented and better-written defenses of capitalism and critiques of socialism.

[14] Two examples of this position are the magazines *Sojourners* and *The Other Side*. Both are highly provocative and clearly biased, taking controversial positions on political issues.

[15] Taken from the title to Conn's book, *Evangelism: Doing Justice and Preaching Grace,* which ". . . is an effort to look at the relation between evangelism and social questions as two sides of the same coin" p. 9.

[16] Cf. E. D. Hirsch, Jr., *The Aims of Interpretation* (Chicago: The University of Chicago Press, 1976) pp. 1–13; Elliott E. Johnson, "Authors' Intention and Biblical Interpretation" in *Hermeneutics, Inerrancy, and the Bible,* edited by Earl D. Radmacher and Robert D. Preus (Grand Rapids: Zondervan Publishing House, 1984), pp. 409–430.

tablishes the best hermeneutical controls on our usage of the text. Obviously this is not easy in the best of cases, because we are so far from the original picture. This step requires full use of traditional Evangelical hermeneutics while at the same time understanding the cultural and ideological preunderstandings which we bring to the text.[17] The North American and the outcast seminarian or pastor of India can come to the same passage and see similar emphases. They will also see radically distinct themes emerging from the Scriptures. But both must seek for the original authorial intent and meaning *before* going on to application. Don Carson, editor of an excellent work with authors from diverse cultural backgrounds, is very helpful when he notes that a careful comprehension of preunderstandings can lead to an "improved hermeneutical self-criticism."[18]

One must also seek to understand the contemporary significance based on the authorial intent. What the author had in mind must guide our understanding of application and contextualization. This becomes an exciting adventure when we begin to see and judge our presuppositions as we come to the Scriptures. We can attempt to free ourselves and the Scriptures when we allow them to speak for themselves, for they have untapped wealth that we tend to lock in due to our cultural matrix limitations.

The Move From Theory to Praxis

Again, what we do depends on our perspective and commitment to social justice and liberation, and whether we are oriented to social service or social action and transformation.[19] What to one may be liberation could be slavery to another. Within Nicaragua today some Christian leaders see the Sandinistas as liberation from Somoza bondage, but others fear that the revolution has gone sour,

---

[17] Cf. Bernard Ramm, *Protestant Biblical Interpretation,* 3d. ed. (Grand Rapids: Baker Book House, 1970), a classic text in Evangelical institutions; also D. A. Carson's chapter in the work he edited *Biblical Interpretation and the Church: Text and Context* (Exeter: The Paternoster Press, 1984), pp. 11–29.

[18] Carson, *Biblical Interpretation and the Church: Text and Context,* p. 13.

[19] *Grand Rapids Report: Evangelism and Social Responsibility,* pp. 43–44.

swapping one oppressive system for another. It is very easy to lay all the blame for the developments within Nicaragua on the unfortunate American foreign policy, but this reductionism denies the original Marxist ideological framework and intent of the Sandinista leadership.

Risking simplification, here are some alternative approaches to the expression of social justice and liberation. In the first place, one can opt for macro changes of the society. The macro or structural transformation can come two ways. One is violent and seeks for radical revolutionary change at whatever the cost to the previous regime, the national infrastructure, or the people. The second type of macro change can be sought through nonviolent, progressive and democratic changes of the society. Some "first worlders" find this structural change absurd, but they tend to see through the lens of their own democratic traditions where the "revolution" has taken place hundreds of years before. This is not the case in many countries of the two-thirds world, where revolutions are current history and where constitutions are being rewritten. This type of participation is part of social action.

A second alternative is the micro change within the system, with a view of reform, providing smaller models of social justice and liberation. These programs of social service will probably touch a more limited sector of the population, but they can be seen as patterns for the greater regional or national community. Here is where we must come to grips with the three stages of change: from relief to development to transformation. The first two stages are easy to understand. In relief you give a hungry person a fish to eat, but in development you teach him to fish and help him provide a place in which to fish. However, beyond these two comes transformation: the search for ownership of the fishing pond, the distribution system for his products, and even a national structure. Yet this illustration does not express the complexity of the problems faced in our shrinking world of interdependence.

There is yet another combination for change; and that is one which harnesses evangelism, discipleship, and church planting into an integral program of church growth. Here the spiritual dimensions are coupled with the concern for the social implications of the gospel so that biblical priorities are sustained. During 1984 a national congress on church growth was held in Guatemala with an original focus on the numerical aspect of the churches. But the North American agency that organized the event was challenged to change the focus from statistics to holistic church growth in a context where the church was growing rapidly, a new constitution was being written for the nation, and where Evangelicals were beginning to exercise political influences beyond their church walls.[20]

Yet another approach to social justice and liberation calls for escapism, for a denial of the balance between Bread and breads. It is nonbiblical, unrealistic, and a negation of responsibility beyond personal comfort.

What Shall We Do to Respond?

We must avoid mere activism for activism's sake, much of which surges out of guilt and false motives. Here are four suggestions.

First, we must recover and demonstrate a Christian conscientization regarding our topic: this means becoming critically aware of the nature of the crises regarding social justice and liberation in the world.[21] It will also require an uncomfortable reworking of priorities as those of us who are more privileged economically see the inhuman human situation within the USA—some rural areas and the inner cities—and outside our national boundaries. We hear and see the tragic pictures of famine and starvation in Africa, revolutions in Central America, and the incredible mass of humanity in Asia. Let us see people as Christ would see them, helpless sheep without shepherds, needing Bread and bread. We must not allow the secular worlds to co-opt this topic, for it is not one that belongs to them alone.

Secondly, as committed Evangelicals we must follow through from conscientization to biblical studies on social justice and libera-

---

[20] Amanecer '84 was the national congress on church growth held in Guatemala with speakers who represented the statistical focus, as well as the holistic elements.

[21] Paulo Freire, *Pedagogy of the Oppressed* (New York: Seabury Press, 1970). Freire is the man who introduced the term *conscientization* into formal usage.

tion. This will require biblical contextualization on the topic, as well as a healthy and respectful dialogue between Evangelical academics and committed activists. It will mean opening up our theological categories to allow entry of newer themes into the traditional systematics. It will mean opening up a dialogue between biblical thinkers from the wealthy and poor nations. There is a need for more volumes such as those edited by Robert G. Clouse on war and poverty, but which will also include capable writers from the two-thirds world.[22]

A third stage demands a serious assessment of spiritual and economic priorities within the North American Evangelical community. Personal, family, church, and institutional objectives and budgets must come under new scrutiny. Particularly the edifice complex which has infected churches and institutions must be brought under the lordship of Christ. The same must be said of the vast sums swallowed up in overhead expenses. The American church and its members are very much a part of the mystique which values pragmatism and, more dangerously, materialism. Jefferson certainly would not be considered a Christian, but he spoke prophetically in words engraved in his monument in Washington, D.C.: "Indeed I tremble for my country when I reflect that God is just." We might apply this to the American churches also. Where is the teaching on light and salt in a corrupt and corrupting society? More articles such as Philip Yancey's on money need to be circulated, hopefully to produce changes in our life-styles.[23]

Yet a fourth step challenges us to commit greater resources to meet social justice and liberation needs in our interdependent world. The American church must sense her responsibility as the national government cuts down on federal relief and aid programs. Why not clearer thinking on the refugees in our midst as nearby "hidden peoples" to be reached biblically? How much longer will we ignore the corrosive, inner-city needs of America?

The same must be done in greater scope for the rest of the world.

---

[22] Robert Clouse has edited two key books: *Wealth and Poverty: Four Christian Views of Economics* (Downers Grove: Inter-Varsity Press, 1984) and *War: Four Christian Views* (Downers Grove: Inter-Varsity Press, 1981).

[23] Philip Yancey in "Learning to Live with Money," *Christianity Today* (December 14, 1984), pp. 30–42.

Churches could adopt special projects that combine evangelism and church planting with relief and development. One recent report from Mali affirms that the "phenomenal growth in the Christian population of the Nonkon district of Mali may be attributed to the Christian witness of food relief programs in the drought-plagued regions. . . ." Here social action emerges as a manifestation of and partner of evangelism.[24]

But beyond these micro approaches, we must stimulate believers to become creatively and biblically involved in deeper aspects of social justice and liberation in their countries. This is particularly true in lands where the country's future is up for grabs or is in the process of major change. We must stimulate mutual respect, as well as a Christian concept of vocations. John Stott writes that "Jesus Christ calls all His disciples to 'ministry,' that is, to service." Today we have a vast set of career options to be exercised and,

> In all these spheres, and many others besides, it is possible for Christians to interpret their lifework christianly, and to see it neither as a necessary evil (necessary, that is, for survival), nor even as a useful place in which to evangelize or make money for evangelism, but as their Christian vocation, as the way Christ has called them to spend their lives in his service. Further, a part of their calling will be to seek to maintain Christ's standards of justice, righteousness, honesty, human dignity and compassion in a society which no longer accepts them.[25]

One final step calls for us to be sensitive to the dangers of promoting social justice and liberation. We must not confuse or lose our biblical priorities, particularly the mandate of Christ to take the gospel of redeeming grace to lost mankind. To bring a more just society, and raise the living standard of oppressed people, without also giving them a basis for forgiveness, true peace, and everlasting life, would leave people still in bondage to sin and hell. The Lau-

---

[24] "Missionary New Service," EMIS (February 1, 1985).
[25] John R. W. Stott, *Christian Mission in the Modern World* (Downers Grove: Inter-Varsity Press, 1975), pp. 31–32.

sanne Covenant warns us that "... reconciliation with man is not
reconciliation with God, nor is social action evangelism, nor is political liberation salvation. ..."[26] There is no substitute for the eternal, saving message of Christ, with the centrality of the Word of
God and a high view of its nature and authority. Our concept of social justice and liberation springs from our concept of the Scriptures
and its themes. It is an expression of our Christian commitment,
whether seen as a bridge to, partner of, or result of evangelism.

Some Final Observations

The prime concern in this chapter has been to demonstrate an
Evangelical response to the cry for social justice and liberation. It is
a statement made by one who has lived for twenty-seven years
within the context of Central America and who has struggled biblically, practically and personally with this burning issue.

We yearn for full social justice and liberation for all human
beings today, but we realize that no system—Marxist, socialist, mo-
narchical, or democratic—will provide the ideal. With the Apostle
Paul we seek for the deliverance for all creation and meanwhile will
struggle to live the gospel in our lives and spheres of influence. We
must seek social justice and true liberation within all peaceful
means at hand. This is not to bring in the kingdom by human
means, but rather to demonstrate the truly Christian cultural values
which are a model of kingdom ethics and life-style.

The issue comes back to evangelism. For finally, the hearts of
men and women must be changed to create a genuine society of
righteousness. The Great Commandment to love can only be realized through obedience to the Great Commission to make disciples
of Jesus. This will never be easy in the twisted state of a fallen race.
All the hosts of hell will seek to destroy, or at least divert, the gospel
witness. Here is the real struggle today for human dignity, and it
must be faced courageously.

Meanwhile, we trust the sovereign God of history who with the
eternal Godhead created this planet, man and culture. This mighty

---

[26] *Let the Earth Hear His Voice,* pp. 4–5.

God will send His Son to establish His kingdom of justice on earth and will rule with a rod of iron and creative economic practices. But even there we will see rebellion. The final solution to social justice and liberation will come only in the new heaven and the new earth, in the living presence of the eternal God. *Maranatha!*

Questions for Thought

1. Why does evangelism create a concern for social justice and true liberation?

2. What is the fallacy of liberation theology in its popular Marxist form?

3. In practical terms, what are some ways that social justice and liberationism can come today? Which option seems best?

4. How does the Bible establish guidelines for us to follow? How are they determined?

5. In what sense is the kingdom of Christ both present and future?

5

The Contextualization of the Gospel

David J. Hesselgrave

David J. Hesselgrave is Professor of Mission in the School of World Mission and Evangelism at Trinity Evangelical Divinity School. He received a diploma in theology from the seminary, then went on to earn a Bachelor of Arts degree in philosophy from the University of Minnesota, as well as the Master of Arts and Doctor of Philosophy degrees in rhetoric and communication.

Dr. Hesselgrave has served as pastor in Radisson, Wisconsin, and Saint Paul, Minnesota, and was, for twelve years, an Evangelical Free Church missionary in Japan. He taught at the Evangelical Free Church Bible Institute of Japan and at the University of Minnesota before joining the faculty at Trinity in 1965. In 1972 he was visiting professor at Evangelical Theological College in Hong Kong, and he held a similar post at the Asian Theological Seminary in Manila in 1973. He has lectured and led seminars in over forty countries.

A contributor to many missions periodicals, Dr. Hesselgrave has authored *Communicating Christ Cross-Culturally, Planting Churches Cross-Culturally,* and *Counseling Cross-Culturally.* He is a coauthor of the books *I Believe: Studies in Christian Doctrine, Evangelical Free Church History and Missions,* and *What in the World Has Gotten Into the Church?* In addition, he is the editor of three books and a contributor to numerous other volumes.

Dr. Hesselgrave is a member of the American Society of Missiology; a member of the Association of Evangelical Professors of Mission, of which he is past president; and is on the boards of a number of missions-related organizations.

Products of Our Culture

Someone has said that our culture is our mother. There is some truth to that. In a very real sense we are rocked in her cradle, nourished at her table and brought up under her watchful eye. In fact, try as we may, we cannot escape her influence. However far we may travel in our later years, the tendency will be to reflect her world view, speak her language and display her values. In spite of the change that true conversion brings, even so radical an experience as Christian conversion will change this state of affairs only incompletely and only over a period of time.

It is also true that "Mother Culture" herself changes—sometimes imperceptibly slowly and sometimes with great rapidity. (It would be more correct to say "Mother Cultures" because there are many of them, so we will take that into account from here on.) In our time whichever of the world's myriad "Mother Cultures" might be "ours," the likelihood is that she is changing rapidly and dramatically. The cultures of the Western world are in process of abandoning the world view and value system that has been the heritage of Judeo-Christianity. They are becoming more and more *post-Christian.* With few exceptions outside the animistic areas, the non-Western cultures have largely retained their traditional religions such as Hinduism, Buddhism, Shintoism and Islam. Impacted by Western technology and secularism, they have changed but not primarily in a Christian direction. They remain *pre-Christian.*

Now to the extent that our culture is our "mother" and that recent culture change has made Western cultures post-Christian and left non-Western cultures pre-Christian, it follows that Christian evangelists everywhere must adjust their sights. No longer can evangelists in the West assume that the majority of their hearers accept the authority of the Bible, understand all that is really important about spiritual things, and need only to be persuaded to act upon what they already know and believe. And no longer can evangelists in Africa and Asia assume that the majority of their hearers will rightly interpret a simple rehearsal of the Christian gospel, readily acknowledge its superiority, and intelligently respond by abandoning the old ways and adopting the "Christian way."[1]

Culture, Culture Change and Contextualization

This brings us to the concept of *contextualization*. The word itself is comparatively new having been introduced in a 1972 report of the Theological Education Fund of the World Council of Churches.[2] In using it, early exponents such as Nikos Nissiotis, Shoki Coe and Aharon Sapsezian sought to encourage third-world theologians especially to analyze the cultural and sociopolitical contexts in which they live and then to "do theology" from that contextual perspective rather than starting with the Scriptures and historic creeds of the church. The fact that the word *contextualization* was coined by liberal theologians and accorded a meaning that suited their predisposition to a sociopolitical interpretation of the Christian mission resulted in considerable resistance to the term on the part of Evangelicals.[3] Let us elaborate on this briefly.

Contextualization, of course, is derived from the word *context.* The Latin word for "context" means to weave or join together. From time immemorial interpretation theory has recognized that the larger discourse and the shorter passage or word must be considered together in order to determine the meaning of the latter. Similarly, classical rhetorical theory recognized that it is necessary that the speaker adapt to his audience in order to be effective. Aristotle, for example, observed that it was one thing to praise Athenians among Athenians and quite another thing to praise Athenians

---

[1] For a more complete presentation of this subject, see David J. Hesselgrave, *Communicating Christ Cross-Culturally* (Grand Rapids: Zondervan, 1978). Also see Eugene A. Nida, *Message and Mission: The Communication of the Christian Faith* (New York: Harper & Row, 1960); and Bruce J. Nichols, *Contextualization: A Theology of Gospel and Culture* (Downers Grove: Inter-Varsity Press, 1979).

[2] Theological Education Fund, *Ministry in Context* (Bromley, Kent, United Kingdom: New Life Press, 1972).

[3] Bruce C. E. Fleming, *Contextualization of Theology: An Evangelical Assessment* (Pasadena, CA: William Carey Library, 1980).

in any other context! The TEF call for contextualization would
have met with deserved approval on the part of Evangelicals if the
call would have been to a new appreciation of the fact that Christian communicators must sensitively adapt their message to hearers
in the context of their own culture. In fact, very likely the challenge
to encourage third-world theologians to "do theology" in such a
way as to answer the questions and problems posed by their own
culture also would have met with approval. The difficulty was that
the initiators of the term went much further than this. According to
them, the contextualizer is supposed to discern what God is saying
and doing by immersing himself in the struggles and concerns of
people (especially the poor) in their various cultural contexts, and
then contextualize the gospel with reference to Scripture. It was this
stipulated definition which undercut the authority of the Scriptures
by consigning them to a secondary role in the contextualization process to which Evangelicals primarily objected.[4]

It is possible, then, to reject the stipulated definition proposed by
the TEF while recognizing the necessity of "weaving together" the
message and cultural context. We can use the term in a more ge-
neric sense to signify the kind of adaptation that makes the message
"meaning-full" to people who have been—or are being—"moth-
ered" (the technical term is *enculturated*) in a culture different from
that of the Christian communicator. This kind of contextualization
is reflected in the best of missionary literature and in the Scripture
itself. Our Lord Jesus dialogued very differently with the Jewish
Pharisee Nicodemus than He did with the Samaritan woman (her
name is graciously omitted from the record). The Apostle Paul
preached very differently in the synagogue in Pisidian Antioch, the
streets of Lystra, and the Areopagus in Athens.

Furthermore, unless the gospel *is* contextualized (in this latter
sense of the word) we run the risk of communicating a truncated or
distorted gospel to more and more people in both Western and
non-Western cultures. That is so because the vast majority of people interpret the gospel message in the light of the world view and
value system of their own culture (which they tend to accept uncrit-

---

[4] Morris A. Inch, *Doing Theology Across Cultures* (Grand Rapids: Baker
Book House, 1982), pp. 17–24.

ically) rather than the world view of the Christian evangelist (which they may not understand at all).

Evangelicals, then, must prepare to face this contextualization issue. If the astute theologian Donald Bloesch is correct, the world is not becoming increasingly Christian. It is becoming increasingly pagan.[5] We can anticipate, then, that unbiblical contextualization proposals will not magically disappear; nor will the need for a contextualization that is faithful to the Scriptures in either Western or Eastern cultures diminish. Our response must be both negative and positive—the avoidance of erroneous contextualization proposals and the adoption of approaches that make the gospel meaningful and relevant.

Let us assume here that the task of countering the most flagrant liberal contextualization proposals (such as the TEF proposal referred to above) falls primarily to Evangelical theologians and missiologists. Great responsibilities still remain for the evangelist— negative and positive responsibilities.

Dangers to Avoid

Oversimplification is one pitfall. Many evangelists will be tempted to downgrade the importance of culture thereby avoiding the hard questions. After all, the easy option is to assume that Western cultures have not changed that much and that most Westerners readily *understand* the gospel even though they may not readily *accept* it. As a matter of fact, it is easy to assume that if we reduce the gospel to a few simple statements and translate them into the local language, it will be meaningful to the people of *any* culture. All that remains is for the evangelist to persuade his hearers to act in accordance with their understanding.

The facts are very different. The farther one's "Mother Culture" takes one from the world view of the Bible—as revealed from Genesis to Revelation—the more carefully and patiently the "larger picture" must be "filled in" if the gospel is to be meaningful and

[5] Donald G. Bloesch, *Crumbling Foundations: Death and Rebirth in an Age of Upheaval* (Grand Rapids: Zondervan Publishing House, Academic Books, 1984).

compelling. West and East, people need a contextualized gospel today more than ever. We do Christ and His church no service by oversimplifying the complexity of our task.

On the other hand, oversophistication is also a snare. There is a tendency on the part of some to invest culture with so much importance that culture becomes a *determinative factor* in both divine revelation and human communication. In this view, meaning does not inhere in words; it exists only in people. Words are not all that important; meanings are all-important. As concerns the Bible, it is the meanings which are inspired. The words are inspired only in a secondary sense as a kind of by-product of the inspiration of meaning. This being the case, the best interpreter of the Scriptures is not the scholar who is expert in the history and language of the Bible, but the scholar who has mastered culture and anthropology. The anthropologist is the one who is able to ascertain the meaning and impact that the words had on the original hearers or readers in the cultures of, for example, pre-exilic Judah or first-century Corinth.

According to this suborthodox view, when it comes to contextualizing the biblical message for the people of our own day, we must first determine the impact that the biblical words had on the original hearers in their culture and then strive to use contemporary language in such a way as to reproduce (as far as possible) the same response in our hearers in their particular culture. If, for example, the people in an Indonesian culture highly prize pigs and use them in their sacrifices and John intended to convey a positive appreciation of Jesus when he introduced Him as the Lamb of God (John 1:29) in first century Jewish culture, then gospel communication may be better served by the pig analogy than by the lamb analogy according to this view. In fact, entire passages of the Scriptures may require similar revision.

Now we must hasten to insist that something is to be gained when we look at language and communication in this way. There have been positive gains in moving from the nineteenth-century, static view of language to the much more dynamic view of the twentieth century. But great risks are also involved. In making gospel communication so complex we run the risk of discouragement and even despair at the practical level. At least one learned journal dedicated to gospel contextualization was withdrawn because it promoted confusion instead of clarity. But even more alarming is the possibility of undercutting the authority of the Bible as consisting of the very words of God. It must be remembered that our Lord claimed divine authority for the words of Scripture, not just the ideas. And as astute as any twentieth-century examiner might be, he does not have access to the inner workings of first-century evangelists and their auditors. He has access only to their words.[6]

Pursue a Biblical Contextualization

Having spoken of that which we should carefully avoid in contemporary evangelism, we can now speak of that which we should wholeheartedly pursue. To do this we must return to the definition of contextualization which we have adopted here—namely, the attempt to undertake the kind of adaptation in our communication of the gospel that will make the gospel message meaningful to people whose culture is different from our own. The classic examples of this approach come from the Scriptures themselves. We have already called attention to our Lord Jesus and the Apostle Paul in this connection. Equally instructive is a comparison of the abilities and ministries of Peter and Paul.

Peter was called to preach the gospel primarily to the Jews while Paul's ministry was primarily to the Gentiles (Galatians 2:7–8). Quite obviously, Peter had not been prepared for Paul's kind of ministry. In his own culture he was a most effective communicator. But when moving among people of another culture, he experienced tremendous difficulties (Acts 10; Galatians 2:11–21). If one compares the preaching of Paul with that of Peter, it becomes apparent

---

[6] Note that even though this approach is advocated by some Evangelicals, if carried too far its results are not dissimilar to those invited by the contextualization proposals of the TEF discussed previously. In the TEF case, properly trained theologians are supposed to be able to discern the Divine will by participating in human struggles for justice. In the case before us, bicultural anthropologists are deemed able to discern the impact of the biblical message on the original hearers and on that basis determine the real meaning of the text and valid contextualizations for today.

that Paul adapted his message to his audiences in a way that would have been impossible for Peter. Nevertheless, both believed and preached the same gospel (Galatians 1:9–12). In fact, it is imperative that we take note of the fact that Paul's fundamental concern was that the gospel not be truncated in order to appeal either to Christian leaders on the one hand or to pagan Gentiles on the other. Biblical contextualization preserves a pure gospel while communicating it in a culturally meaningful way.

A Contextualized Proclamation Today

There are, of course, many facets of the contextualization of the gospel. In the paragraphs that remain let us examine two facets that will be of particular importance to contemporary evangelists—the first having to do with its proclamation and the second having to do with its invitation.[7]

In post-Christian Western cultures an increasing number of people are becoming *naturalists.* God (in the Judeo-Christian sense) and spirits are not "really there." Man evolved out of something (who knows what?) over a period of millions of years; and in more millions of years (cross your fingers) will continue to evolve. (Some naturalists might be tempted to say "will evolve into heaven knows what," but of course there is no heaven in their world view.)

Evangelists in Western cultures who fail to contextualize with the foregoing in mind will find themselves communicating to fewer and fewer people. Rather than assuming that people are interested in God, they will have to assume that people are primarily interested in themselves for men are alone in the world. Rather than assuming that people accept the authority of the Bible, they will have to assume that people think of it as just another (good) book. Rather than presupposing that people understand sin, they will do better to presuppose that most people think that sin (whatever it was)

---

[7] Helpful suggestions in reaching different cultures and people groups, from a broad international perspective, are compiled in the *Lausanne Occasional Papers* (Wheaton: Lausanne Committee for World Evangelization, 1980–81). Of particular interest will be the various Thailand Reports of the Consultation on World Evangelization held at Pattaya, Thailand, June 16–27, 1980.

went out with the Victorian Age and that whatever it is that might be wrong with the human race should have another name. This is just the beginning, of course. But it points in the direction of a contextualized proclamation of the gospel in Western cultures today.

Pre-Christian cultures of the non-Western world present us with quite a different picture although naturalism and secularism have greatly influenced many of them. In these cultures we encounter Indian or Chinese or Muslim or tribal views of the world, as the case may be. Once again—and to a degree many of us have not previously realized—contextualization is necessary if the gospel is to be rightly understood.

Think of the classic Indian world view, for example. That view is almost the antithesis of Western naturalism. The universe houses myriads of deities and spirit beings, some of whom periodically appear in human form. Man is fundamentally a spiritual being with an *atman* or soul at the core of his being. Man's fundamental problem is bad *karma* which binds him to seemingly endless rebirths and ignorance of the true nature of things. And what is the "true nature of things"? It is that the "really real" is not man or nature or even the various gods and spirits. All of these are illusory. Behind them all is the Brahman from which all has evolved and to which all will eventually return. Meanwhile there is this seemingly interminable cycle of births and rebirths except for the miniscule number of holy men who achieve enlightenment and oneness with the Brahman "ahead of schedule."

Imagine for a moment that *your* cultural "mother" is India. How would you react to the message "You must be born again"? What would be so unusual about the incarnation of Christ? Why would you hesitate to accept another deity or another incarnation of deity (just to make sure)? Is not sin just another name for bad *karma?* And what is so holy about these Christians (especially Christian evangelists from the West) anyway? They certainly appear to be overly concerned with hairstyles, fashionable clothing and a variety of *materials* ranging from stereo amplifiers to flashy guitars!

Can there be any doubt that an uncontextualized proclamation of the gospel actually distorts the gospel? No. The best that can be said for it is that it results from unintentional sins of omission.

Contextualizing the Invitation

Almost as important to evangelism as gospel proclamation is the gospel invitation. Evangelists often echo Paul's words: "We try to persuade men" (2 Corinthians 5:11 NIV) and "[it is] as though God were making his appeal through us" (2 Corinthians 5:20 NIV). But though these verses should end some arguments among Christians as to the appropriateness of persuasion evangelism, they do not answer questions about the kind of appeal that should be made and how it should be made. In part such questions can only be answered in the light of culture.

For example, post-Christian Western cultures (particularly that of the United States) have retained a commitment to individualism and decision making (*any* decision is better than none) as basic values. To these values they have added an inordinate preoccupation with the self. A pre-Christian culture such as Chinese culture, on the other hand, is committed to communalism and "indecision" (Confucius advised delaying decisions as long as possible). The self is subordinated to the group—especially the extended family.

Obviously, inattention to the need for a contextualized approach to the appeal to repent and believe the gospel will tend to result in invitations that are dictated in large measure by one's own culture. The North American evangelist, therefore, will tend to extend his invitation to individuals (ignoring the family group) and will tend to press for an immediate decision (downgrading potential misunderstandings). And he will tend to do this irrespective of whether his audience is composed of Americans or Chinese.

An awareness of the desirability of contextualized appeals, on the other hand, will result in change. Of course, if the evangelist is not sensitive to Scripture as well as culture, the change will not likely be for the good. He may, for example, neglect Christ's appeal to deny oneself and follow Him while emphasizing self-esteem, self-improvement, self-fulfillment, and self-actualization—prevalent themes and values in current American psychology and popular culture. On the one hand, if sensitive to the Scriptures *and* to culture, he will make a more balanced appeal in American culture.

And, should he have the privilege of presenting the gospel to Chinese, he may well allow more time for his hearers to gain a true understanding of the gospel, and he may emphasize the possibility (and desirability) of entire families coming to Christ as did the households of Cornelius, Lydia and the jailer of Philippi.

Two Certainties

In conclusion, it is important that we underscore two great truths of the sacred Scriptures. In the first place, God's Word will not fail. The Scriptures cannot be broken. All will be fulfilled. This remains true whether or not we take the time and effort to defend it from the eroding effects of unwarranted contextualization approaches. Nevertheless, the clear command to "contend earnestly for the faith which was once for all delivered to the saints" (Jude 3 NAS) and the clear implication of Paul's strenuous defense of a pure gospel (Galatians 1:20) indicate that we should expose any contextualization attempts that undermine the authority of the Scriptures and the gospel.

In the second place, God's plan will not fail. The gospel will be preached to all nations (Matthew 12:14). A people will be called out from all tribes and tongues and peoples and nations (Revelation 5:9). The Holy Spirit will convince people of sin, righteousness and judgment (John 16:8). Nevertheless, the clear command is that we preach the gospel to all creatures (Mark 16:15), and the clear implication of the adaptations made by Jesus and the apostles indicates that we should employ contextualization techniques that enhance the clarity and relevance of gospel communication. Alan Tippett has said it well:

> The greatest methodological issue faced by the Christian mission in our day is how to carry out the Great Commission in a multi-cultural world, with a gospel that is both truly Christian in content and culturally significant in form.[8]

---

[8] Quoted by James O. Buswell, III, "Contextualization: is it only a new word for indigenization?" *Evangelical Missions Quarterly* 14 (January, 1978), p. 13.

The challenge to maintain the authority and message of the biblical gospel while responding more sensitively and meaningfully to cultural differences has never been more needful than it is in our day. And, considering the ease with which we cross most other barriers, whether geographical or ethnic, it has never been more appropriate. Communicated faithfully and meaningfully, the gospel of Christ is truly good news for all men everywhere.

Questions for Thought

1. What do we mean by a pre-Christian culture? A post-Christian culture? Name one culture that you think fits into each category and give reasons for your choice.

2. Give two diverse definitions of the word *contextualization.*

3. Is it possible to oversimplify the gospel? In what sense?

4. What is wrong with translating "Lamb of God" (John 1:29) into "Pig of God" in a culture where, unlike ours, pigs are highly valued and sheep are unknown?

5. Who do you think was the better contextualizer, Peter or Paul? Provide some illustrations that help to validate your choice.

6. What possible pitfalls does contemporary psychology pose for the contextualization of the gospel in American culture?

6

Power Encounter With the Demonic

Timothy M. Warner

Timothy Warner, former missionary to Africa and President of Fort Wayne Bible College, came to Trinity Evangelical Divinity School in 1980. He is presently the Director of the Doctor of Missiology and Doctor of Ministry programs, and also teaches in the School of World Mission and Evangelism.

His educational background includes an A.B. in religion from Taylor University, a Master of Divinity in English Bible from New York Theological Seminary and a Master of Arts in religious education from New York University. The Doctor of Education degree was awarded by Indiana University.

He has written *The Place of General Education in Bible College Curriculum,* the biography *S. A. Witmer: Beloved Educator,* and is a contributing author to *Facing Facts in Modern Missions,* as well as a contributor to numerous Christian periodicals. During his seminary training, he pastored churches in New York, and continues to serve on various boards in the Missionary Church.

Awareness of Spiritual Warfare

Some student workers in Colombia, South America, were having a very fruitful ministry. They were well-prepared except in one area. "We ... faced the whole issue of the occult," the husband writes.

Practical knowledge in this area was just not part of our academic preparation! As we began to lead people to the Lord, we discovered that nearly nine out of ten had prob-

lems in this area, for one reason or another. The Lord led
a missionary into our lives who had the experience we
didn't. We started taking our people to her, she'd pray,
and God would free them.[1]

This type of encounter with the power of Satan has been common
in certain parts of the world, but it is becoming increasingly common in North America as well. It is one of the issues which the
church will need to take seriously as it plans its evangelistic strategy
for the future. The popularity of Eastern mystical religions, the
rapid rise of occult activity, the adoption of Satanism by rock
groups, the fascination with psychic phenomena by spiritually
starved secularists, and many other developments in our day mean
that an increasing number of people in our society have opened
themselves to demonic influences. We need to be prepared to face
this type of problem in both the evangelistic encounter and in the
discipleship process.

Evangelism always involves power encounter in the sense that it
is the bringing of men and women from the "power of Satan to
God" (Acts 26:18 NIV). There is a sense in which the whole Christian life is a power encounter. Peter wrote to the Christians of his
day that their "enemy the devil prowls around like a roaring lion
looking for someone to devour." For that reason they were to be
"self-controlled and alert," and were to "resist him, standing firm in
the faith" (1 Peter 5:8–9 NIV).

Unfortunately (and in some cases, even tragically), the average
Christian today has little idea of how to "resist" this adversary; and
pastors and missionaries, like the youth workers in Colombia, are
not equipped to teach "practical knowledge" in this area. There is a
veritable vacuum in most theological education on this topic.

Why This Vacuum?

There are a number of reasons for this. One of them is that the
excesses of the church in the Middle Ages apparently led the re-

---

[1] "A Time of Reaping" in *Latin America Evangelist* (July–September, 1983),
p. 6.

formers to back off from the elaborate exorcism rites being practiced by the Roman Catholic Church at that time. In getting rid of
their excesses, however, they failed to provide a biblical way to deal
with the problem. Alan Tippet says, "They reaffirmed the power of
evil, but left believers disarmed before the old enemy." He goes on
to say, "I question whether the Christian churches [today] have
provided their members with an adequate faith for this kind of
ever-increasing confrontation with spirit forces."[2]

This inadequacy is reinforced by the influence of Western culture
which has become increasingly secular in its world view. While
most of the world yet to be won for Christ assumes that spirits or
spiritual powers are behind most of what happens in the world, the
educated Westerner assumes that spirits are incidental to our understanding of the world, if, indeed, they exist at all.

To test the accuracy of this, even for Evangelical Christians, we
have only to ask ourselves, When do we modify our conduct more
readily? When important people are present or when significant
spirits are present—even God, the Holy Spirit?

The fact is, however, that we are involved in conflict with the
"prince of this world," to use Jesus' title for Satan, whether we want
to be or not; and this is especially true when we begin actively to
invade his kingdom through evangelism.

Personal Level of Encounter

This encounter takes place on two levels. On the first level the
forces of Satan are on the initiative, attacking the person involved
in evangelism or any other form of Christian ministry. This is why
the Scriptures speak of defensive armor for the Christian and of the
necessity to resist or to stand against Satan's attacks.

On the second level God's servants are on the initiative, attacking
the forces of Satan. This is the ministry level. This begins with
evangelism and extends to the direct encounter with demons.

One cannot expect to invade Satan's territory without resistance

---

[2] "Spirit Possession as It Relates to Culture and Religion" in John W. Montgomery, ed., *Demon Possession* (Minneapolis: Bethany House Publishers, 1976),
pp. 166–68.

from Satan, and evangelism is such an invasion. It is sometimes assumed that there is an automatic protection from Satanic (demonic) attack for a spiritual person involved in Christian service. There is little basis for such belief. All the warnings against Satanic attack are addressed to Christians. On the other hand, there is clear evidence that Jesus was the object of such attacks throughout His life. He demonstrated that there are adequate resources to successfully resist such attacks. But to say that the believer has resources to resist the enemy is quite different from saying that he has automatic protection from attacks.

One of Satan's primary strategies for Christians is to neutralize them in this struggle. If he can succeed in keeping them from effective witness, he may well be content to leave them alone as far as active attacks may be concerned. But he has too much at stake in their becoming active soul winners to allow that process to go on unchallenged. He knows that his chances of sidetracking them entirely are not good; so he is content simply to reduce them to ineffectiveness in life and witness.

Many people have wondered why, when they began to get serious about living for Christ, their problems increased rather than lessened. The answer is that Satan simply cannot afford to allow such growth to take place without resistance. So, if we are going to engage in ministry which is going to do damage to Satan's kingdom and is going to bring glory to God, we had better be prepared for spiritual combat.

His attacks may come in different areas at different times. One often meets the enemy first in the area of prayer. This is the Christian's "big gun." S. D. Gordon says, "Prayer is striking the winning blow at the concealed enemy. Service is gathering up the results of that blow among the men we see and touch."[3] If that is true, and I believe it is, it is no wonder that Christians find true intercession to be difficult. Satan is certain to try to silence our big gun.

But if that doesn't work, he will try other tactics, such as attacks on our bodies, on our emotions, or in the area of our relationships. He may take what are normal problems and intensify them to

---

[3] S. D. Gordon, *Quiet Talks on Prayer* (New York: Grosset and Dunlap, 1941), p. 21.

levels that defy the usual physical and spiritual disciplines. At that point we need to know how to use "the weapons of our warfare" (2 Corinthians 10:4).

Some Illustrations

Some years ago a missionary teacher was sent home from the field because she had become so debilitated that she could not carry on her ministry. She went to the best doctors and clinics she could find, but after two years of this with no improvement, she finally decided to give up. Her debility was such that she made up her mind to put her Bible on the shelf and stop trying to be a Christian—even to stop living.

The morning she was to implement this, the Lord said to her, *"Why don't you fast and pray and cast them out?"* No one had suggested that her problem could have a demonic source even though she had been in an area where Satan's power was very evident. She decided to give it a try even though she had no experience or training in such things.

To make a long story short, she wrote out the commands for the evil spirits troubling her to leave "in the name of Jesus Who shed His blood on Calvary for me," and she read them every thirty minutes during the day. She now testifies, "I was delivered that day.... The change was so great I could hardly take it."[4]

As my wife and I have become more involved in ministering to persons with problems caused by demons, we have come under attack in various ways. At one point we began to have compulsively critical thoughts about each other. We had worked our way through almost thirty years of married life with the usual communication problems, but never was it like this. We did not even talk about this problem with each other.

After a week or so of this, we both came to the conclusion, still without talking to each other about it, that the thoughts were an attack of the enemy. We commanded him to leave, and immediately

---

[4] "Victory Over the Powers of Darkness" (Goldenrod, FL: World Wide Keswick, n.d.)

the compulsive thoughts were gone. Such encounters must be recognized for what they are and resisted "standing firm in the faith."

Attacking the Enemy

The second level of encounter puts the Christian on the initiative against the enemy. Through witness and ministry we invade the world over which Satan holds dominion, and we do so under the authority of the King of kings. This begins with a life which bears witness to His power to redeem. It continues with active witness in which the truth of the gospel is verbalized to those who are outside the kingdom over which Christ is Lord.

In the minds of too many of us in the Western world, this is the extent of ministry. We have been taught to proclaim the message of Christ, but we have not learned to demonstrate the power of Christ in all areas of life. To be sure, there is power involved in conversion and living a victorious Christian life, but the areas of victory are often quite limited.

In many parts of the world, however, (and increasingly so in places in the West) people are much more power conscious than they are truth conscious. In such places, we may preach a very logical and convincing message by Western standards, but our hearers are unimpressed. Let them see Christian power displayed in relation to the spirit world of which they live in great fear, however, and they will "hear" the message more clearly than our words alone could ever make it. Donald Jacobs contends that "most people in the non-Western world convert to another faith because of seeking more power."[5]

This is not to imply that truth is unimportant. Everything must be based on and tested by the truth of the Scriptures. It is to say, however, that truth proclaimed is often not enough. This is why Jesus, when He commissioned the apostles, "appointed twelve ... that they might be with him and that he might send them out to preach

---

[5] Cited by John Newport in J. W. Montgomery, ed., *Demon Possession* (Minneapolis: Bethany House Publishers, 1976), p. 334.

and to have authority to drive out demons" (Mark 3:14 NIV, italics mine). That is why He said to the seventy, "I have given you authority to trample on snakes and scorpions and to overcome all the power of the enemy" (Luke 10:19 NIV). He always linked demonstration of power with His proclamation of the kingdom, and we never find Him commanding His disciples to preach the kingdom without also telling them to heal the sick and cast out demons.

Modern Examples

This principle is what lies behind such accounts as that of the ministry of OMF International in West Kalimantan. "It seemed that the 'god of this world,' " writes Robert Peterson, "had complete control over these subjects. Well-meaning observers assured us it was impossible to expect any spiritual results under such conditions." And for fifteen years there were very few results from their evangelistic ministries.

A dramatic change came about, however, and in the next few years more than 1,500 moved "from darkness to light, and from the power of Satan to God." The field chairman evaluated the situation this way:

> We believe it is not just coincidental that when the Lord's servants commenced openly to challenge the power of darkness and, in the name of our victorious Lord, commanded the demons to come out of the possessed ones, the gates of hell began to yield and captives were set free.[6]

Similar accounts could be given from other areas of the world. The experience of the church in China today is a significant illustration of this. The China Prayer Letter reports that "many of the spiritual battles in China are being fought with acts of prayer and healing. The demonic powers are being confronted just at those points where they have had the most effect."[7] Among the rules

---

[6] Robert Peterson, *Are Demons for Real?* (Chicago: Moody Press, 1972), pp. 8, 9.
[7] "China Prayer Letter," May, 1983, p. 3.

established by the government for the church in China is "Don't pray for the sick and don't cast out demons." The reason for such a rule is that these demonstrations of power are part of the regular ministry of the house churches, and they are very effective in the evangelistic outreach of the church.

Many with whom I have spoken recently agree that the key to reaching some of the very resistant peoples around the world is power encounter. In many places we have proclaimed the message, but we have not demonstrated the power of Christ. Until that happens, some people will not "hear" the gospel.

Personal Preparation for Battle

An aggressive invasion of Satan's territory through evangelism must begin with personal preparation. We must first examine our own world view to determine how much we expect to happen through spiritual power—both God's power and Satan's power. This will involve an admission on our part that we have been more deeply influenced by the secular philosophy of the society around us than we would like to admit.

Our standard Evangelical theology readily acknowledges that our God is all-powerful and that there are such beings as angels and demons. In actual ministry, however, we demonstrate that we do not believe that God's power is very functional in everyday life or that angels and demons have much to do with life here on earth. Our world view tells us that men and machines, not spirits, make things happen. The idea that demons or angels or even the Holy Spirit is very active in this "natural" world has, at best, been reserved for the theology books and, at worst, relegated to the realm of superstition. We fear the possible excesses of too much emphasis on the supranatural or the suprarational, and we back off to the opposite extreme of denying the possibility of spirit activity which Jesus and the early church took for granted.

We need to begin by acknowledging our fear of power encounter and our tendency to take refuge in a position which denies, in practice if not in theory, that there are demonic powers at work in our world, and which therefore ignores the power and authority available to the Christian to gain victory over them. The prevalent fear of anything demonic is testimony to this.

Our self-examination on this issue will involve an admission that we have been more deeply influenced by the secular philosophies around us than we would like to admit. While we profess great faith in God's power to operate today in the human realm, the fact is that we set our daily priorities and carry on our activities as though it is men who get things done, not God.

Most of us will have a great deal of personal homework to do in finding out what it means to be "filled" with the Holy Spirit. It is obvious that the Spirit is not finding very much freedom to express His power through most of us.

The armor of Ephesians 6 will need to become more functional than it has been for many. It is not enough to be able to name the parts; we must be able to demonstrate its effectiveness in spiritual combat. Power encounter sometimes involves resisting Satan's attacks on us with the shield of faith, but sometimes it involves using the sword to take the offensive against him.

Jesus told the seventy that He was giving them authority over all the power of the enemy (Luke 10:19), and that same authority is given to us today. We need to learn how to use that authority against the same enemy of which Jesus spoke to the early disciples.

Large segments of the church around the world have learned their privileges as children of God and regularly use this authority in the realms of healing and dealing with demons. The church in Latin America, China, and Indonesia are examples of this. Christians from such places find our fear of the supranatural to be very strange. They read the Bible and simply believe what they read rather than trying to find an explanation for it that does not require acceptance of supranatural power as a necessary factor for us today.

If S. D. Gordon is right that prayer strikes the winning blow against the enemy, then prayer will have to have a great deal more consideration in our setting of evangelistic strategies, and we will have to learn new ways of praying—ways that include the exercise of spiritual authority against our enemy. Intercessors will have to recognize that when they enter their prayer closets they enter the primary battlefield, and they need to be prepared to do battle with the enemy.

It may be very significant that Paul prescribes the putting on of the Christian armor in Ephesians 6 especially for those who will do what he leads to at the end of that passage—pray! At the end of such a strong admonition to put on spiritual armor, one would expect to hear him say, "Now fight!" And in a sense he does, because that is what real intercession is. As Jesus taught in the parable of the unjust judge, persistence in prayer is not needed to overcome any reluctance on the part of God. It is needed because we have an adversary. Daniel learned that truth through his experience. The reason he had to fast and pray for twenty-one days was the activity of a spiritual enemy, not the reluctance of God to answer his prayer (Daniel 10:12–14).

Binding the God of This World

If Satan is the god of this world, it follows that he will have his underlings assigned to various parts of the world. He is not omnipresent; so he must carry on his work through the host of demons who serve him. It seems safe to assume that just as there was a "prince of Persia" who withstood the angelic messenger sent with the answer to Daniel's prayer in Daniel 10, so there are "princes" in charge of other geographical areas.

For example, a young missionary about to enter a new village of Indians in Canada was counseled by an older worker, "When one enters a new area untouched by the gospel, one must be prepared to face the ruling spirit or guardian angel of that place." The new missionary went to the village, and it wasn't long before he met the spirit in charge. First his wife became ill and had to be flown out. Next it was his son. Then he tells of the decisive encounter.

> One night after midnight I was praying, standing with my back to the stove for extra warmth, when I heard a frightening groaning coming down the stove pipe behind me. At the same time I was gripped palpably across the chest and throat and a great weight settled upon my frame. I was able to stagger to a nearby chair. Immediately the words of the old missionary came to mind, "You may have to

face the ruling angel of that village." So I said, "All right, Satan, you guardian angel of Borchet, let's have it out. Jesus Christ sent me here; I might die but I am not leaving, and with the Lord are the issues of death."

I continued in this vein for about half an hour, claiming the legal victory of Calvary, and all the while gasping for breath. I proved the truth of James 4:7: "Resist the devil and he will flee from you."

That was the decisive battle. There were many more, but we stayed on in joy and victory for the next four years.[8]

Every Christian needs to know how to resist the devil, but it is imperative that a pioneer evangelist know how to take the initiative against him. Such an evangelist in Papua, New Guinea, tells of being totally frustrated in his attempt to preach in a new village until he learned to bind the spirits of the village before he went there. When he did that, the witnessing situation was entirely different.

Other types of encounter may involve the destruction of occult materials (Acts 19:19), prayer (1 Kings 18), healing (Acts 14:8–18), open confrontation (Acts 13:4–12), and the actual casting out of demons (Acts 16:16–18).

More Than Conquerors

This issue of encounter with demonic forces is one which has understandably been avoided by large segments of the church. For most of my life, I was among those who steered clear of any such involvement. My missionary ministry in Africa and my more recent experiences at home have convinced me that we can no longer afford this luxury. By doing so we live below our privileges in the gospel; we forfeit a ministry to persons who desperately need the power available to them through the victory of Christ; and we give Satan the satisfaction of seeing God deprived of the glory which is rightfully His.

---

[8] *Attack from the Spirit World* (Wheaton: Tyndale, 1973), p. 127.

The way we deal with this issue is a reflection of the conflict in which we are engaged. Satan's strategy is to twist and pervert truth in order to accomplish his purposes. He does this by getting Christians to give him more credit than he deserves, finding him behind everything that happens, or by ignoring him to the extent that they almost never see his involvement in the affairs of life. He is the one who wins the encounter when we allow ourselves to go to either of these extremes.

I was a chaplain's assistant with infantry troops in the Second World War; so I know what war is. On the basis of that experience, I would hope that no one would ever have to be involved in war again. And on the basis of my experience in dealing with demonized people, I would hope that no one would have to do that either. The fact is, however, that we are in spiritual conflict whether we like it or not; and we need to learn to be good soldiers.

Finally, two other things need to be said before we leave this brief treatment of a large subject. First, the reader is urged to pursue the subject further in the literature available on the subject.[9] The second thing is that one needs to be thoroughly convinced of the victory of Christ over Satan and all of his hosts. Fear of demons is an expression of unbelief. They are not to be taken lightly, to be sure. They are powerful beings, and they must be respected for what they are. But the Scriptures leave no room for doubt about their defeat. The purpose of Christ's coming was to destroy Satan and his works (1 John 3:8; Hebrews 2:14), and at the cross Jesus did just that (Colossians 2:15).

The proclamation of the message of the cross and the demonstration of the power of the cross are an unbeatable combination in evangelism.

---

[9] Some helpful readings on this subject include: Mark I. Bubeck, *The Adversary* (Chicago: Moody Press, 1974); Kurt E. Koch, *Occult Bondage and Deliverance* (Grand Rapids: Kregel Publications); John MacMillan, *The Authority of the Believer* (Harrisburg: Christian Publications, n.d.); Oswald J. Sanders, *Satan Is No Myth* (Chicago: Moody Press, 1975); Merrill F. Unger, *Demons in the World Today* (Wheaton: Tyndale House, 1976); and by the same author, *What Demons Can Do to Saints* (Chicago: Moody Press, 1977).

Questions for Thought

1. What is the relationship between the proclamation of truth and the demonstration of power in the ministry of Jesus, especially in the Gospel of Mark?

2. Consider the nature and results of the power encounters in the Book of Acts.

3. What is the principle issue at stake in the conflict between God and Satan (Isaiah 14:12–14; 2 Thessalonians 2:4), and how is this reflected in Satan's attacks on people, especially God's children?

4. Paul says that he is not ignorant of Satan's devices (2 Corinthians 2:11). What are Satan's devices?

5. Paul also says that "the weapons of our warfare are . . . mighty before God to the casting down of strong holds" (2 Corinthians 10:4). What are these weapons, and how do we become skillful in using them?

7

Self-esteem and the Pursuit of Fulfillment

Gary R. Collins

Gary R. Collins, Professor of Psychology and former Chairman of the Division of Pastoral Counseling and Psychology at Trinity Evangelical Divinity School, came to Trinity in 1969 after teaching at Portland State University, Bethel College and Conwell School of Theology. He is a frequent lecturer in colleges, pastors' conferences and church meetings across America and around the world.

A native of Canada, Dr. Collins has the Bachelor of Arts degree from McMaster University and a Master of Arts from the University of Toronto. In 1963 he received the Ph.D. in clinical psychology from Purdue University, and has done post-graduate work at the University of London and at Western Baptist Seminary.

Dr. Collins has written a number of books including *Christian Counseling, How to be a People Helper, The Rebuilding of Psychology, Beyond Easy Believism,* and *The Magnificent Mind.* In addition, he contributes to periodicals such as *Leadership, Christian Herald* and the *Journal of Psychology and Theology.* Dr. Collins is a member of the American Psychological Association and the American Scientific Affiliation, having served as president of the latter organization in 1974.

A New Phenomenon

I have often wondered what happened to Mr. Green. Thirty-five years ago, when he was my Sunday school teacher, he may have been middle-aged, but to me now he looked like a very old man. He never mentioned a wife, so I assume he was a widower who lived with his grown son. Mr. Green wasn't a leader in our church, and it is possible that few people even knew him.

But I knew him, and I respected him greatly, probably because he cared so much about the kids in his Sunday school class. When I went to the university he promised to pray for me (he probably did), and although he had little education himself, Mr. Green expressed one concern about college that I have never forgotten.

"Don't get too involved with psychology," he warned. "It can be very harmful for your spiritual growth."

In the years that followed, as I felt led to pursue graduate studies in psychology, I watched some of my fellow students who claimed to be Christians but who had never heard Mr. Green's warning. One by one these people abandoned the faith and gave themselves completely to what some have called "the new religion of psychology."

Mr. Green could never have predicted how powerful this new religion would become. He could not have known that psychology would become the most popular major among American college students; that in the 1970s more textbooks would be published on psychology than on any other subject; that it would be more difficult for students to be accepted into graduate programs in clinical psychology than to be admitted into medical school; that psychology would take its place in the curriculae of the theological seminaries and become a central theme of innumerable sermon outlines; or that the psychology which was planted in Europe and blossomed in America would quickly rush to take root in almost every part of the world.

The Psychological Religion

Several years ago, about the time when Mr. Green was my Sunday school teacher, Julian Huxley published an explosive little book titled *Religion Without Revelation*.[1] Huxley defined religion as "a way of life" that is based on the belief that "certain things" are sa-

---

[1] Julian Huxley, *Religion Without Revelation* (New York: Mentor, 1957).

cred. There is no need to believe in the supernatural, he wrote. "Religion of the highest and fullest character can co-exist with a complete absence of belief in revelation . . . and of belief in . . . a personal god."

Huxley's views were not unique. Earlier philosophers had agreed with Nietzsche that "God is dead," and some respected theologians were proclaiming the same message. Freud had dismissed religion and religious beliefs as "illusions" and many agreed with psychoanalyst Erich Fromm's secular definition of religion as "any system of thought and action shared by a group which gives the individual a frame of orientation and an object of devotion."[2] Together, humanist philosophy, liberal theology, and secular psychology advanced the view that traditional religion, and especially biblical Christianity, was no longer viable or relevant.

It is not surprising, perhaps, that as traditional religion and the Protestant ethic weakened, people looked to "the psychological expert who claims there is a new scientific standard of behavior to replace fading traditions."[3] Psychology became the new religion. It was a religion that promised relief from psychological suffering, guidance in the affairs of life, a worship of human potential,[4] and freedom from the need to believe in revelation or the supernatural. The new psychological religion rejected the concept of sin,[5] and maintained, instead, that maturity, happiness, and even freedom from guilt would come to those who believe in self-determination, self-actualization, and self-fulfillment.

Within recent years, several perceptive writers have criticized this

---

[2] Erich Fromm, *Psychoanalysis and Religion* (New Haven: Yale University Press, 1950), p. 21.

[3] Martin L. Gross, *The Psychological Society* (New York: Simon and Schuster, 1978), p. 4.

[4] An insightful analysis of this new religion has been published by an evangelical Christian who teaches psychology at New York University. See Paul C. Vitz, *Psychology as Religion: The Cult of Self-Worship* (Grand Rapids: Eerdmans, 1977).

[5] Two powerful voices from within the social sciences challenged this thinking. One was a former President of the American Psychological Association; the other has been widely respected as one of this century's greatest psychiatrists. See O. Hobart Mowrer, *The Crisis in Psychiatry and Religion* (Princeton: Van-Nostrand, 1961), and Karl Menninger, *Whatever Became of Sin?* (New York: Hawthorn, 1973).

subtle "psychological seduction,"[6] but none has written more clearly than Martin Gross, a journalist and social critic who apparently makes no claim to be a Christian. "Never before has a general philosophical system so concerned itself with the *Self*," Gross wrote in *The Psychological Society.* "Never before have so revered self-indulgence. . . . To egocentric modern man, the prospect of *Self* instead of *God* seated at the center of a world philosophical system is exquisitely attractive."[7]

A New Reformation

It is distressing, but probably not surprising, that this "exquisitely attractive" philosophy has seeped into the church. It began, as we have seen, with the more liberal seminaries and churches, but its influence has gone much further.

Nowhere is this better seen than in the philosophy of positive thinking. Initially made popular by the books and preaching of Norman Vincent Peale, the idea is now expressed most eloquently in the worldwide television ministry of Robert Schuller. It has been estimated that on any Sunday morning, more people hear Robert Schuller than any other preacher. With a mixture of showmanship and enthusiasm, Schuller proclaims the essentials of his "New Reformation."[8] This is a theology that says little about self-denial, repentance, or the reality of sin,[9] but puts emphasis instead on "possibility thinking" and the need to build better self-esteem. Schuller believes that self-esteem is "the greatest single need facing the human race today."[10] He writes that

[6] See, for example the previously cited books by Gross and Vitz. The term *psychological seduction* was used by William Kirk Kilpatrick, *Psychological Seduction: The Failure of Modern Psychology* (Nashville: Nelson, 1983). See also Bernie Zilbergeld, *The Shrinking of America: Myths of Psychological Change* (Boston: Little, Brown, 1983).
[7] Gross, *Psychological Society* p. 14.
[8] Robert H. Schuller, *Self-esteem: The New Reformation* (Waco: Word, 1982).
[9] For an interview with Schuller and a critique of his views on sin, see the August 10, 1984, issue of *Christianity Today.*
[10] Schuller, *Self-esteem,* p. 19.

prayer, worship, and well-thought-out sermons will not produce morally strong and spiritually exciting Christians if they fail to produce self-confident, inwardly secure, nondefensive, integrated persons. . . . All of the problems facing the church will find healing answers if we start with and do not get distracted at any time from meeting every person's deepest need—his hunger for self-esteem, self-worth, and personal dignity.[11]

Schuller argues, correctly, I believe, that if we are to communicate the gospel message, we must make it relevant to the people we are trying to reach. Many of these are pleasure-seeking, psychologically sophisticated individuals who don't understand us and who are not much inclined to hear what we say. Most contemporary people, at least in our culture, struggle with feelings of low self-esteem and a lack of personal fulfillment. Few are likely to pay attention to a hell-fire-and-brimstone, "worm theology" type of sermon. In our age of television, is it likely that more people will be reached with the kind of showmanship that Schuller so effectively demonstrates?

In their zeal to reach others for Christ, people like Robert Schuller have emphasized correctly that only Christ can bring true self-esteem and real personal fulfillment. But the gospel also teaches that salvation, and hence true fulfillment, only comes to those who confess verbally that Jesus is Lord, and who believe that God raised Him from the dead (Romans 10:9). Christ suffered to take away our sin (Hebrews 9:26, 28), and it is only through trusting in Him that we find true joy and hope (Romans 15:13). A message may be filled with hope and possibility thinking, but it is not the gospel message if it ignores or deemphasizes the reality of sin or if it fails to call for repentance and submission to the Lordship of Christ. Even when it is presented in the church, a message that fails to emphasize salvation by grace through faith in Jesus Christ as Lord and Savior, is still a proclamation of man-made psychological religion.

---

[11] Ibid., pp. 26, 35.

Confronting the Challenge

Schuller would answer that his critics are too harsh; that he is striving to reach nonbelievers by speaking to their needs. Whether or not we agree, it is clear that the church has always been faced with the challenge of showing that the gospel is relevant to the age in which we live.

This challenge includes the need to defend the gospel against its accusers and critics. Throughout history, generations of theologians, and apologetists, and ordinary believers have sought to follow Peter's plea that we "always be prepared to give an answer to everyone who asks you to give the reason for the hope that you have. But do this with gentleness and respect, keeping a clear conscience, so that those who speak maliciously against your good behavior in Christ may be ashamed of their slander" (1 Peter 3:15–16 NIV). These words, written centuries ago, certainly apply today as we confront an age of psychology that believes in a gospel of self-esteem and self-fulfillment.

Most Christians would probably agree that "the best apologetic is not a defensive mind-set that sits back and waits for attacks." It is far better to make positive statements about our beliefs—what we believe to be true about God, people, and the universe.[12]

In making our statements, however, we must be aware of the personal struggles that people face and of the "unknown gods" that they worship. The best-selling books of our day are not biblical commentaries and volumes of systematic theology. Instead, people buy books and flock to seminars that deal with stress, love, finances, success, and personal enrichment. Popular writings on self-help psychology sell in the millions and there is great interest in finding answers to the problems of depression, guilt, insecurity, anxiety, sexual nonfulfillment, marital tension, and a host of other issues that previous generations might have kept well-hidden. If we ignore these contemporary issues and fail to show how the gospel meets

---

[12] William Dyrness, *Christian Apologetics in a World Community* (Downers Grove: Inter-Varsity Press, 1983).

such human needs, then we are in danger of hiding the gospel from those who are lost.

Some sincere Christian leaders try to ignore psychology; others are uninformed about its teaching but critical of its influence and conclusions. These are extreme positions, as unbalanced as the views of those who are so captivated by psychology that they embrace it enthusiastically but without recognizing its limits and weaknesses.

In spite of its limits and weaknesses, modern psychology has captured the popular thinking of our day and proposed answers to contemporary human dilemmas. Psychological analyses have also provided convincing arguments to explain away the reality of conversion, prayer, belief in the supernatural, biblical miracles, and almost every variety of religious experience. In the psychology classes that worried my former Sunday school teacher, psychology professors are indoctrinating students with arguments that oppose and attempt to undercut the gospel.

Do we ignore such arguments, or do we join with Christians of all ages to refute those of our contemporaries who are critical of the gospel? Do we pretend that the new psychological religion does not exist, or do we confront it by showing that faith, built on Jesus Christ, is the answer to human needs including the need to find self-esteem and fulfillment?

It will not be easy to develop this new apologetic. Unlike some of the false religions of previous eras, the new psychological religion is not much interested in theology or the defense of personal beliefs. Instead, there is an emphasis on tolerance, individuality, love, goodwill, self-fulfillment, togetherness, personal success, peace, joy, and hope. The traditional focus on truth, belief in God and knowledge of the holy, has been replaced with an emphasis on personal freedom, good feelings and rules for self-management.

More recently, however, many psychologists have been coming to realize that their science cannot explain the meaning of life or death, cannot give ultimate standards for right and wrong, cannot effectively deal with moral dilemmas including guilt, and cannot give lasting hope to the deeply depressed or terminally ill. It should not be assumed that psychologists are flocking to the gospel. Nothing like this is happening or is likely to happen in the near future. Nevertheless, there are minor cracks in the antireligious armor of psychology and there has never been a time like the present for showing the relevance of the gospel to our psychology-saturated age.

Relevance to Evangelism

In spite of the criticisms that one might have of Robert Schuller, most would agree that he has had phenomenal success in understanding and reaching the affluence-seeking, pleasure-oriented, success-motivated nonbelievers who live in his community. These people have psychological needs that Schuller has identified and tried to address with a Christian message. Billy Graham has done the same, although from a more traditional perspective, and with a biblical rather than a psychological gospel.

How does all of this apply to evangelism today?

This chapter has been critical of the field of psychology, but please let me remind you that the criticisms have come from an Evangelical psychologist who seeks to be a devoted follower of Jesus Christ, who believes that the Great Commission is to be taken seriously, but who is devoting his life to the study and teaching of psychology. Of course, contemporary psychology has weaknesses and it is true that many have made it a new religion that opposes the biblical gospel. But when it is subject to the truths of God's Word, and made available to the leading of God's Holy Spirit, psychology can be a valuable tool to help people cope effectively with their problems, to guide them in their movement toward self-esteem, to answer the accusations that come from intellectual critics of religion, and to point people to Jesus Christ who is the ultimate source of personal fulfillment.

A Wholesome Attitude

What, then, should be our attitude towards modern psychology? How do those who believe in the Great Commission respond to the influence of psychology?

First, don't ignore it; instead try to understand it. As every Christian counselor knows, there is much of value that can be learned from the science of psychology—including techniques for understanding and reaching people who are deeply distressed and sometimes filled with complicated jargon. Still, much is easily comprehended and there can be value in reading books or taking courses, especially those that come from trained, competent psychologists who are sympathetic to the Christian message.

Second, don't try to squelch psychology; instead try to evaluate it and learn from it. I ask all of my students to read some of Freud's criticisms of religion. Freud was a nonbeliever, but he was insightful in spotting some of the weaknesses of Christians. Students often find that his conclusions can be helpful for those who want to better understand themselves, their culture, and their critics. Even more valuable have been the writings of Gordon Allport, the late Harvard psychologist. Allport's analysis of mature and immature Christians is both insightful and helpful.[13]

Is it possible that God, in His wisdom, has allowed human beings to discover truths about themselves and about the universe through the study of psychology? If we agree that the answer is "yes," then we can learn from many of the conclusions of psychological research.

Third, don't be enamored by psychology: instead, try to keep it in perspective and build on it. Psychology does not have all the answers to life's problems. Even the most enthusiastic psychologists are likely to agree with that. In spite of its present popularity, psychology must be kept in perspective. It is a helpful field of study that enables us to understand and speak with greater relevance to modern human beings, but it is a field that does not have all the answers.

We must never forget that it is the Holy Spirit who convicts men of sin. It is God's Son, Jesus Christ, who brings ultimate fulfillment and self-esteem to the human beings He created. Often, in His mercy and goodness, He works through imperfect human beings to accomplish His purposes. Sometimes, He graciously works through

---

[13] Gordon Allport, *The Individual and His Religion* (New York: Macmillan, 1950).

the sciences, technologies, evangelistic programs and theologies that He has allowed us to discover and develop, to bring people to Christ and to help them find fulfillment.

Even Mr. Green would not object to that.

Questions for Thought

1. Why has psychology become a new religion to so many people?

2. How does psychology help people solve some of their problems?

3. What are some of the limits and weaknesses in the psychological approach?

4. In light of the behavioral sciences, what place does the supernatural have in religious experience?

5. How are personal freedom and self-fulfillment reconciled with the gospel of the cross?

8

Preaching for Decision

Lloyd Merle Perry

Lloyd Perry, after retiring as Professor of Practical Theology at Trinity Evangelical Divinity School, now occupies the Chair of Pastoral Ministry at Lancaster Bible College. Prior to coming to Trinity, he taught at Aurora College, Northern Baptist Seminary and Gordon Divinity School. An ordained Baptist minister, his leadership in the church as pastor or interim preacher spans more than four decades.

He is a graduate of Gordon College and Gordon Divinity School, has the M.A. degree from Columbia University, and holds three earned doctorates—Th.D. in Practical Theology and Homiletics from Northern Baptist Theological Seminary, the Ph.D. from Northwestern University in Speech Education and Oral Interpretation of Literature, and the D.Min. from McCormick Theological Seminary.

Dr. Perry is a frequent speaker at pastors' conferences, retreats and seminars in the United States and Canada. He has also lectured widely on college and seminary campuses.

Among the more than twenty books he has written or contributed to are *Getting the Church on Target, A Manual for Biblical Preaching, Getting Help from the Bible, Biblical Preaching for Today's World, Revitalizing the Twentieth Century Church,* and *The Wycliffe Handbook of Preaching and Preachers.*

The Evangelistic Sermon

Biblical, evangelistic preaching will always be crucial in reaching souls for the Savior. Churches grow and are especially blessed when

115

high priority is given to this ministry of the Word. That it has been downgraded in many churches gives reason for serious concern.

This form of preaching involves the proclamation of the gospel in such a manner that men and women are called to accept Jesus Christ as personal Savior and Lord. To be sure, all Christian preaching should expect a response of the will, whatever the subject of the sermon. But in the more specialized sense, evangelistic preaching centers upon the redemptive truths of salvation, a message that carries with it the imperative that all persons must repent and believe the gospel. Such preaching is not necessarily any special type of sermon or homiletical method; rather, it is preaching distinguished by the call for commitment to the Son of God who loved us and gave Himself for us.

This passion for lost souls to come to God should shine through an evangelistic message. Yet this does not take away the necessity for responsible preparation. The very urgency of the task demands that the evangelist use every principle of good homiletics.

Dependence Upon the Spirit of God

Most essential, of course, is the preacher's reliance upon the Holy Spirit. Without the Spirit's enablement the whole effort will be utterly fruitless. Paul was well aware of this when he wrote to the Thessalonians, "For our gospel did not come to you in word only, but also in power and in the Holy Spirit and with full conviction" (1 Thessalonians 1:5 NAS). Preachers dare not depend on natural means to produce supernatural results.

The scriptural analogies regarding the Holy Spirit speak to this point. In John 3 He is likened to wind that stirs. In Acts 2 He is likened to fire that purifies. In Isaiah 61 He is likened to oil that invigorates. In Revelation 22 He is likened to water that refreshes. The church today needs evangelistic preaching that will stir, purify, invigorate and refresh. Apart from the Spirit of God at work in the heart and life, the preacher's sermon becomes an echo chamber of meaningless words and irrelevant thoughts. The Holy Spirit is the "Divine Dynamic" who enables the evangelist to be powerful, persuasive and practical.

Not only does the Holy Spirit call and equip the evangelist, but

He also strengthens him for his monumental task. The Spirit of God enables the preacher to discipline his mind and body. He prods the man of God to deeper devotional study and intercessory prayer. He helps him handle the multiplicity of demands on his time and energy that otherwise would inhibit and stunt his ministry and influence for Christ.

The strategic role of the Holy Spirit in the sermonizer's preparation is seen in the ministries He performs. The Holy Spirit is the producer of the evangelist's primary source material, the Word of God. He is the penetrator of the evangelist's understanding, enabling him to properly observe, interpret, apply, and communicate gospel truth. He is the provider of the evangelist's authority. Apart from the divine truth internalized through the indwelling presence and illumination of the Spirit of God, there is no authority in evangelistic preaching.

Know the Audience

The preacher, with the help of the Spirit, must seek to lift his audience to a level where they will be willing and responsive listeners. For this to take place, he should ever keep in mind the nature of the people addressed. By understanding where they are coming from, the evangelist can make his appeal more direct and meaningful in their situation.

Basically there are four types of audiences in terms of their interests and their attitudes toward the speaker, and the ideas included in the presentation.[1] The *apathetic audience* is one which is not interested in the message. The members of it do not believe, oppose or doubt the presentation. They just don't have any interest in it. When such an audience is involved, the physical factors in the speaking situation take on special significance, like removing dis-

---

[1] It is likely that all four types of listeners are in any audience, though one group may predominate. Whatever the complexion of the congregation, however, an evangelistic sermon should be preached to all, even when the group is largely a believing audience. Some will be aroused; some will be convicted; but all will be helped, stimulated and comforted. For a helpful discussion, see David Breed's *Preparing to Preach* (London: Hodder and Stoughton, 1911), pp. 401–13.

tractions from the speaking area or getting the people to sit close to-gether. Stress should be placed upon the unanimity of feeling which exists among the auditors.

The first few minutes of a message are of special importance. It is wise to avoid big abstract generalizations or a long, rambling history of the subject. This includes overelaborate definitions. And whatever you do, do not begin with an apology. An effective introduction will be short, presented with quiet confidence and be characterized by variation in delivery.

The *doubting audience* is one which has not as yet formed definite opinions. They need to see the weight of the data. It is necessary to show the validity of the argument itself without injecting too much of the personality of the speaker. The speaker must be able to talk factually, make predictions, develop theories and draw logical conclusions. He should, also, not present inferences as though they were facts.

Remember, too, that when we are dealing with people all situations present complexities. There is a tendency to overemphasize similarities and overlook differences. We, thus, distort the picture of the world in which we live and make it difficult to see variety as it exists. In dealing with the doubtful audience we should strive to fix the variables by giving the specifics of identification.

When a speaker is dealing with a *hostile audience,* it is helpful to develop a positive response to his bearing as a person. This involves establishing authority to speak. The preacher's vitality, confidence, sincerity, sympathy, kindness and compassion will go far in establishing this credibility. It is essential that respect for the audience be evident by the speaker not being too pompous and patronizing.

A wise preacher in his approach to the hostile audience may emphasize all of the areas in which the speaker and the audience have common interests. Sometimes it may be helpful to begin the message by asking a series of questions to which the audience will give quiet assent within their minds. Or he may approach the audience with absolute candor by stating his purpose openly.

The *believing audience* is often a passive people. This group accepts the position of the speaker, but does not respond to his pleas for acceptance and action. A presentation to such an audience should contain a maximum of illustrations and a minimum of principles. The speaker may make use of visual aids since theoretically every idea can be visualized. He may want to invite audience participation. Illustrations such as anecdotes and examples will reduce fatigue. Without examples, no principles really make sense. The speaker will find it profitable to use comparisons, similes and metaphors. It is helpful to include the telling of details. These are the little details which the average person would tend to overlook.

Style of Sermon

Good sermonic style, especially with reference to the evangelistic sermon, cannot be overemphasized. The evangelist can lose his audience if he is not careful to develop a lucid and articulate mode of expression that crosses all the communication barriers in any given setting. Normally such an approach can be enhanced by getting right to the point of the sermon without camouflaging the real intent with anecdotes and niceties that detract the listener, keeping him from hearing what he came to hear, namely the gospel of Christ.

Simple, nontechnical language will vastly improve the presentation, words that the congregation know well and use frequently. Language should be contemporary, and used in terms of present needs and problems. Jesus employed language that confronted people where they lived and then awakened a positive response.

From introduction to conclusion, the sermon should follow a convincing course of logic. Not only should the objective of the message be clear; there should be a progression of thought leading up to the call for decision. In this sense, the whole sermon has direction by nature of the invitation.

The Call for Decision

Here is the hallmark of evangelistic preaching, or as it is sometimes called, Kerygmatic preaching.[2] It is that part of the message

---

[2] This is the designation employed by H. C. Brown, Jr., in his book *Quest for Reformation Preaching* (Waco: Word, 1968), pp. 140–42.

that issues a challenge to the congregation to act positively upon what the preacher has proclaimed from the Word of God. Daniel Baumann, quoting Clifton J. Allen, offers this definition:

> The invitation is not a gimmick to catch souls. It is not a fetish to insure results. It is not a ritual to confirm orthodoxy. It is simply the call of Christ to confront persons with the offer of his redemption, the demands of his lordship, and the privilege of his service.[3]

Ozora S. Davis expresses the same sentiments, as do almost all the writers in the field of evangelistic and homiletic theory, when he says: "The most important factor ... in the evangelistic sermon is the direct drive for a decision in favor of the message on the part of the hearers."[4] The importance of an invitation is expressed by Leighton Ford:

> I am convinced that the giving of some kind of public invitation to come to Christ is not only theologically correct, but also emotionally sound. Men need this opportunity for expression. The inner decision for Christ is like driving a nail through a board. The open declaration of it is like clinching the nail on the other side, so that it is not easily pulled out. Impression without expression can lead to depression.[5]

Of the many reasons for giving evangelistic invitations, probably biblical precedent is most significant. Our Lord Himself uttered pleadingly, "Come unto me, all ye that labour and are heavy laden, and I will give you rest. Take my yoke upon you, and learn of me; for I am meek and lowly in heart: and ye shall find rest unto your souls" (Matthew 11:28–29). The New Testament record closes with a great invitation: "And the Spirit and the bride say, Come. And let

---

[3] J. Daniel Baumann, *An Introduction to Contemporary Preaching* (Grand Rapids: Baker, 1972), p. 209.

[4] Ozora S. Davis, *Evangelistic Preaching* (New York: Fleming H. Revell, 1921), p. 67.

[5] Leighton Ford, *The Christian Persuader* (New York: Harper and Row, 1966), p. 124.

him that heareth say, Come. And let him that is athirst come; And whosoever will, let him take the water of life freely" (Revelation 22:17). Similarly, the Old Testament prophets pressed for a decision. Hosea, in pleading for the people of the Lord to return to Him and accept His forgiving grace, said, "Take with you words, and return to the Lord: say unto him, 'Take away all iniquity, and receive us graciously' " (Hosea 14:2).

The psychological factor, also, should be considered. Frans D. Whitesell explains, "Emotions aroused and desires stirred will soon pass away unless acted upon at once. Good impulses are harder to generate the second time then they were the first time if the first impulse did not result in action."[6] It might even be claimed that an evangelistic invitation is essential to the well-being of the man in the pew. To bring a person to the point of commitment without giving him an opportunity to make a commitment may be spiritually suicidal.

Certainly the invitation has been an historically proved method of bringing persons to Christ. Almost without exception, the great evangelists, both past and present, have used some form of invitation in securing the results of their messages.[7]

Objections to the Practice

Not all preachers, however, agree that public invitations are helpful. The late Lewis Sperry Chafer thought it an intrusion upon the sovereign work of the Holy Spirit.[8] Likewise, preachers of no less renown than Donald Grey Barnhouse and Martyn Lloyd-Jones, avoided public decision making, considering it to be inconsistent with the doctrines of human inability, grace, and God's election.[9] Seeking to bolster his theological position, though stretching the point, Lloyd-Jones observed that even a

[6] Frans D. Whitesell, *Sixty-Five Ways to Give Evangelistic Invitations* (Grand Rapids: Zondervan, 1945).
[7] A good historical treatment of the public invitation is by R. Alan Streett, *The Effective Invitation* (Old Tappan: Fleming H. Revell, 1984), pp. 55–130.
[8] Lewis Sperry Chafer, *True Evangelism* (Grand Rapids: Zondervan, 1919).
[9] Ford, *The Christian Persuader*, p. 119.

staunch Arminian like John Wesley chose not to make use of the "altar call" method.[10]

Part of the controversy doubtless stems from the play on emotion in the invitational procedure. Perhaps it would be well, for this reason, to distinguish between emotionalism and emotion. Emotionalism is emotion isolated, emotion for emotion's sake. On the other hand, there is a legitimate place for genuine emotion in preaching the gospel. Nothing truly human lacks emotion.[11] Of course, emotion is not everything. We must appeal to the whole person—emotion, intellect, conscience, and will (see Mark 12:30).

Much of the problem, I suspect, comes down to the way an invitation is given. At this point the preacher should be aware of two extremes, on the one hand, having no method of bringing people to Christ, and the opposite danger of overusing one method to the point of "boxing-up" and limiting the Holy Spirit in a preconceived practice.

Varieties of Methods

With sensitivity, then, one must carefully choose the particular method used. Probably the least offensive is the decision-within-the-heart invitation. This appeal is made quite apart from any outward display, and is usually implicit in the closing prayer, wherein the preacher asks the Lord to help the people practice the truth of the message.

The pray-it-through invitation is another approach. Here the evangelist asks for no visible response, but exhorts those who have been deeply touched to go home and pray over the message until they have made their peace with God.

Or an invitation to discuss the message might be given. This was the method of Dr. James Reid, who invited his congregation to the church hall after his sermon to encourage dialogue. Both the saved and unsaved could ask the pastor, either at the close of the service

---

[10] Martyn Lloyd-Jones, *Preaching and Preachers* (Grand Rapids: Zondervan, 1972), p. 270. An excellent review of Lloyd-Jones's position is in R. Alan Streett, pp. 131–138.

[11] Ford, *The Christian Persuader*, pp. 122–23.

or during the week, to talk over their decision and receive more counsel.

Inviting people to sign a card also offers many options. The preacher may urge persons to register their decision on the card, then hand it to the pastor or usher after the service. This information then is used in follow-up.

Raising the hand or standing affords another way to indicate commitment. Sometimes the appeal may be to come forward as a gesture of decision. Those responding may be directed to an inquiry room, where trained leaders are waiting to pray with them and offer spiritual guidance; or the call can be to the altar, where respondents kneel in supplication before the Lord.

There is no end to variety in how an invitation can be extended.[12] The minister will want to ponder carefully the method most appropriate in his particular situation.

Truth of the Message

In light of the urgency for decision, it may be well to keep in mind various motivations for action. George Sweazy suggests some twenty appeals—to the sense of sin, dread of impersonal forces, lost assurances, anxiety, boredom, self-perplexity, death, loneliness, the sense of something lacking, hunger for truth, the missing significance of God, mistrust of life, inner conflict, resentment of material domination, eagerness for a better world, the appeal of the heroic, the craving for brotherhood, love of home and family, admiration for Jesus Christ, and the power of the cross.[13] To these appeals V. L. Stanfield adds the basic drives inherent in individuals, such as self-preservation; personal happiness; recognition; security; freedom; adventure; and satisfaction.[14]

---

[12] Frans D. Whitesell discusses sixty-five ways to give evangelistic invitations in his book. Other very helpful suggestions will be found in R. Alan Streett, pp. 151–220; and Roy J. Fish, *Giving a Good Invitation* (Nashville: Broadman, 1974).

[13] George E. Sweazy, *Effective Evangelism: The Greatest Work in the World* (New York: Harper and Row, 1953), pp. 60–69.

[14] V. L. Stanfield, *Effective Evangelistic Preaching* (Grand Rapids: Baker, 1965), p. 32.

Ultimately, however, the decision is precipitated by the truth of the message. It is not the kind of appeal, nor any methodology of invitation, that should invoke response. Rather it is the nature of the gospel itself that calls for action—the amazing fact that God Himself, the Creator and Lord of the universe, has personally intervened in human history, and through the mighty conquest of Jesus Christ, made a way whereby everyone who believes on Him shall not perish but have everlasting life (John 3:16). Confronting this truth brings us all to account. Before the blood-red cross of Calvary no one can remain neutral. How Christ is lifted up in all the glory of His grace, finally, will be the measure of any evangelistic sermon.

More real gospel preaching in the power of the Spirit should characterize our churches today. Not that every sermon must be addressed to unbelievers, for most worship services are attended by Christians needing to be built up in the faith. Nor is it necessary that an invitation for public decision be extended all the time. Often customs and tastes of the audience make private forms of response more appropriate. Still the opportunity for all people to come to Christ, whatever their need, should be conveyed in every message.

Such preaching requires the best that is in us. There can be no quarter with sin if we are to hold forth God's holy Word, and keep our perspective adjusted toward eternity rather than bound by time. We dare not confront others with the claims of Christ until our own lives are yielded to His control.

It was January, 1930, that Walter Vivian of CBS was checking the equipment which had been installed to carry the message of King George of England to the British navy through the world. In that last-minute inspection a break in the wires was discovered. There was no time for it to be repaired. With one of his hands on the end of each of the two segments of wire, he allowed 250 volts of electricity to go through him so that the King's message could be transmitted. He came out of the experience with burned hands, but the King's message went through.

So may it be with us in transmitting the King of Heaven's message to the lost. We may have to pay a price. But whatever the cost, however difficult the circumstances, let us be about the business of bringing souls to Jesus before night settles in.

Questions for Thought

1. What constitutes an evangelistic sermon?

2. Why is an invitation to receive Christ inherent in the gospel?

3. If the assumption is accepted that the Holy Spirit works through the speaker in extending an evangelistic invitation, what does the Holy Spirit do?

4. How should the form of an invitation be changed depending upon the type of audience?

5. In your experience, what methods of appealing for decision have been most effective in preaching? Why?

9

The Great Commission Life-style

Robert E. Coleman

Robert E. Coleman is Professor of Evangelism as well as Director of the School of World Mission and Evangelism and Chairman of the Department of Mission and Evangelism at Trinity Evangelical Divinity School. He is a graduate of Southwestern University, Asbury Theological Seminary, Princeton Theological Seminary, and received the Ph.D. from the University of Iowa.

A Methodist minister, he served as a pastor until joining the faculty of Asbury Theological Seminary, where he taught until his appointment at Trinity. Apart from his teaching responsibilities, he frequently speaks at colleges and seminaries, church conferences and evangelistic meetings at home and abroad.

Dr. Coleman is president of Christian Outreach, a service organization committed to discipleship resource development. He serves as chairman of the North American Lausanne Committee for World Evangelization, and is past president of the Academy for Evangelism in Theological Education. He has authored more than a dozen books including *The Master Plan of Evangelism* which is now in its fortieth printing. Translations of one or more of his books are published, or in the process of publication, in more than seventy languages.

Getting on Target

An old Kentucky mountaineer, looking back upon his life, mused: "I'd rather chase a rabbit, and not 'ketch' him; than chase a skunk, and 'ketch' him."

His homely expression may have lacked sophistication, but his point was clear. What is gained if we succeed in a task that is not worth the effort? Were this thinking applied to evangelism, I am afraid that many of us would be found wanting. There is plenty going on, to be sure, but is our activity accomplishing the objective set forth by our Lord? Are disciples being made who grow in the character of Christ and become involved in His mission to the world?

Facing this question provokes us to look realistically at the lasting fruit of our evangelistic endeavors. All too many persons who make decisions for Christ soon fall away or, at least, show little progress in sainthood. Even those who grow stalwart in their faith often seem unable to make the gospel relevant to the world in which they live. There is no power in witness, no overflow of love. Critics are especially quick to point out that large accessions to church membership in our generation do not appear to have had a corresponding impact on the morality of society. Concern about this disparity, and the whole issue of spiritual formation, has occasioned renewed interest in discipleship.

Here is the focus of Christ's Great Commission: "Go therefore and make disciples of all the nations, baptizing them in the name of the Father and of the Son and of the Holy Spirit, teaching them to observe all things that I have commanded you" (Matthew 28:19–20, NKJV). The mission is to reach "all nations," meaning all the peoples of the earth, an emphasis consistent with other accounts of Jesus' parting commission.[1] This will happen through "making disciples" which, as the only verb in the original text, gives direction to the participles "go," "baptizing" and "teaching." There is no virtue in just traveling far and wide, seeing how busy we can be in the Lord's work. The only reason for going anywhere is to make disciples. Similarly, the evangelistic imperative to preach the gospel, bringing believers into baptism, has its justification in discipleship; just as teaching has its direction in the building up of Christlike disciples. The whole thrust of the Commission, giving validity to every effort, is the discipling of nations.

A disciple designates one who learns, a pupil, as in the sense of an

---

[1] Note the statements of Jesus in Mark 16:15; Luke 24:47–48; Acts 1:8; John 20:21; cf. 17:18.

apprentice. A disciple of Christ, thus, is one who learns of Him. Such a person is more than a convert, though turning to the Savior in repentance and faith certainly is the point where new life begins. But disciples do not stop with conversion; they keep moving on with Christ, ever seeking to know more of His grace and glory.

Here is the genius of His strategy to win the world, raising up a holy people who will praise Him forever. Disciples, by nature, develop in the likeness of their Lord, and in the process, become participants in His ministry, thereby reproducing the cycle of growth. By making this the focal concern, Jesus assures an ever-enlarging working force, ultimately reaching the ends of the earth with the gospel.

Disciples are to live by the same rule that governed the life of Christ. This is what the Great Commission is all about. It simply enunciates a strategy always implicit in His life-style. Just as He had ordered His life on earth, now we are to follow His example.

Interpreting the Commission

To understand what this means, we must look closely at the way Jesus made disciples. He is Himself the interpretation of the Command. Adaptation of Christ's methods must be made to our situation today, of course, but principles inherent in His way of life establish guidelines for disciples to follow in every age and culture.[2]

We are soon made aware that He lived by a completely different value system from that of the world. Renouncing His own rights, He made Himself of no reputation, taking the form of a servant. He bore our sorrows, carried our griefs, and, finally, accepted in His body the judgment of our sin. The worldlings who watched Him die on the cross said the truth, when in derision they cried, "Look at. Him! He said He came to save others. Why, He can't even save Himself" (cf., Mark 15:29–31; Matthew 27:39–42; Luke 23:35–37).

---

[2] My book, *The Master Plan of Evangelism* (Old Tappan: Fleming H. Revell, 1963, 1964) is an attempt to focus principles in Jesus' life-style. Also, Carl Wilson's study is very helpful, *With Christ in the School of Discipling Building* (Grand Rapids: Zondervan, 1976). An older and larger work, still in print, is the classic *The Training of the Twelve* by A. B. Bruce (New Canaan, CT: Keats, 1979, 1871).

What the mocking crowd failed to understand was that He had not come to save Himself; He came to save us. He "came to seek and to save the lost" (see Luke 19:10). He came not to be served, but to serve, and "to give His life a ransom for many" (Matthew 20:28 NAS; Mark 10:45). What a contrast to the aspirations of this world!

In His servant role, Jesus went about doing good, compassionately responding to the cry of the wandering multitudes. Most people were friendly, but blinded by materialism and self-centeredness, their comprehension of His message was very superficial. What made the situation more pathetic, those persons who were in privileged positions to lead the people, like the priests or scribes, were themselves blind and lost. This was the heartbreak of His ministry. Everywhere Jesus went there were people reaching out for help, but there was no one to lead them. It was obvious that unless spiritual leadership could be raised up—laborers with the heart and mind of Christ—there was no way the waiting harvest could be gathered (Matthew 9:36–38).

So while manifesting love to the multitudes, Jesus sought to cultivate those who someday would lead them. They were called to follow Him. As their numbers grew, He chose twelve to be with Him. Peter, James and John seemed to have had an even-closer relationship. Response to His continuing ministry resulted in increasing numbers of persons who believed on Him, eventually numbering about 500. The growth, however, never detracted from His attention to a small group of disciples around Him.

For the better part of three years, they lived and worked side by side. It was like a family, learning and growing together. In this close association, the disciples were able to see Christ's teaching come alive in daily experiences. Evangelism, like every other aspect of His ministry, was not a mere doctrine; it was a way of life.

As they learned how to assume responsibility, He got them involved in things suited to their gifts. First ministries were small, unassuming tasks, like providing for His hospitality or assisting in distribution of food to the hungry people. The work assignments increased with their developing self-confidence and competence. Before long they were sent out to do much the same kind of work Jesus was doing: visiting, healing, teaching, preaching, and through it all, making disciples.

Jesus would check up to see how they were coming along, building in them a sense of accountability. Problems were dealt with when they came up. Though their progress was painfully slow, especially in comprehending the meaning of His cross, He kept them moving toward His goal. That vision was the ultimate discipling of the nations, and the coming of the kingdom of God.

His concern is nowhere more apparent than in His prayers. Continually He lifts up His disciples, beseeching the Father that the purpose of their lives be fulfilled.[3] When they are overwhelmed by fear, as in the hours before His crucifixion, He holds on for them. Beyond their faltering faith, Jesus envisioned how "through their word" the world would come to believe on Him whom the Father sent, and be one with Him in eternal love (John 17:20–26). That He could have such faith in these beaten, cowed, bewildered disciples leaves us breathless with wonder.[4] Yet that is what discipleship takes.

Jesus did not come in His incarnate body to evangelize the world; He came to offer the atoning sacrifice—to make it possible for the world to be saved. But on His way to Calvary, He concentrated His ministry upon making disciples, teaching them His manner of life, and then commissioning them to go forth in His name to gather the harvest.

To this end they were promised the power of His Spirit, "Another" like Himself, who would continue the work of Christ through them (John 14:12, 16). He would "guide them into truth"; He would show them things to come; He would help them in prayer; and through it all, He would glorify the Son (see John 16:13–14). Indeed, by His presence, Jesus actually would be with

[3] The best example is seen in the High Priestly prayer of Jesus, recorded in John 17. As the largest recorded discourse of our Lord in prayer, it is probably the best insight we have into the mind of Christ. A brief summary of His communion in prayer may be found in my book, *The Mind of the Master* (Old Tappan: Fleming H. Revell, 1977), pp. 37–52.

[4] One of the twelve, of course, the son of perdition, betrayed him, "that the Scriptures might be fulfilled," a fact alluded to in the prayer (John 17:12). Why Jesus would lose Judas, something which He knew from the beginning, raises some profound questions that will have to await a full explanation on the other side of eternity. But, at least, I can see in it a comforting providence, for had they all turned out perfectly, considering my own failures, it would have been more difficult for me to identify with His discipling ministry.

them "always, even unto the end of the age" (see Matthew 28:20). That's why the Great Commission can be fulfilled: the Spirit of Christ lives it out through His disciples.

Practiced by the Early Church

The promise becomes evident as the 120 disciples at Pentecost, filled with the Spirit, begin boldly to bear witness to their reigning Lord. Multitudes hear the message, and when an explanation is given by Peter, about 3,000 people are saved, more in one day than Jesus Himself had won in over three years of ministry. Every day thereafter others are added to the church, as the Christians cease not to spread the good news in the Temple, in the streets, and from house to house (Acts 2:47; 5:42). Persecution only serves to force the disciples into new areas of harvest, and within a generation, the church is planted throughout the Roman Empire.

It is an amazing record of the Spirit reproducing the Christ life. Although some local congregations lose the vision which gave them birth, and, doubtless, many individual Christians fall below their privileges of grace, on the whole, the New Testament church displays the purity and power of her Lord. Those looking on from the outside, observing the bold witness of the disciples, seeing their transparent love, had to admit that "they had been with Jesus" (Acts 4:13).

What also becomes apparent is the similarity of their ministry life-style. That which was confined largely to the Body of Jesus in the gospels is now diffused through His mystical body, the church. Of course, as the witness moves quickly into new and diverse cultures, the strategy takes on a variety of forms—it is contextualized in ever-changing situations. But the basic pattern of Christ's ministry remains the same.[5]

There is His continuing outreach to the multitudes, accompanied

---

[5] A definitive work on Jesus' life-style flowing through the Acts has yet to be written, though principles of His discipling will be noted in various treatments of the apostolic church. One practical application of the text with this in mind is Leroy Elms' *Disciples in Action* (Wheaton: Victor, 1981).

by signs and wonders, with attention centering on persons who seem most receptive to the gospel. Those who desire to know more of Christ are gathered with the apostles or elders, where they continue to grow in grace and knowledge. Brotherly concern, generosity, discipline and prayer mark their fellowship. In this community of trust, they learn the dynamics of sharing their life with others. Spirit-filled leaders give supervision and training. Problems that arise are dealt with realistically, and become stepping stones to ever greater growth. Nothing can permanently defeat them, not the anger of mobs or the frustrations of daily irritations, but like rivers borne along with a loud, rushing sound, they go on their way rejoicing in the triumph of their Lord.

The book of Acts really has no conclusion. The narrative breaks off by reporting that the work was continuing "with all confidence" (Acts 28:31). That is the way it should be, for we are still living in the age of harvest, and it will not end until disciples have been made of all nations, and the King returns in glory.

Confirmed Through Church History

To a remarkable degree, the life-style of the Great Commission continued to characterize the persecuted and impoverished Christians for more than 300 years. However, as the church gained in wordly prestige, eventually being recognized as the state religion of Rome in the fourth century, the apostolic pattern noticeably declined. Through the ensuing Dark Ages, it survived in the simple discipline of a faithful remnant, especially in some religious orders, but, generally, vital discipleship was choked by rigid ecclesiastical policies and spiritual apathy.

With the Protestant Reformation came renewed concern for New Testament Christianity. The Anabaptists especially sought to restore the primitive witness. When the church became embroiled with scholastic disputation, the great seventeenth and eighteenth century Evangelical revivals brought discipleship into greater prominence. From these awakenings missionaries scattered over the earth, and in many areas the churches which they established followed a Great Commission pattern. One example would be the formation and rapid growth of the early Methodist Church in America, a movement which in recent years, sadly, has largely lost its momentum.

As I view the contemporary scene, wherever the fires of evangelism burn brightly in the church, principles of Jesus' life-style can be discerned. Probably the most outstanding example comes out of Communist China. Those who are in a position to know what is going on estimate that there are now 30 million to 50 million followers of Christ in that land, which represents possibly an eightfold increase within two decades.[6] What makes this growth so impressive is that the Chinese Christians do not have many of the ingredients for growth enjoyed in the Western world: for the most part, they do not have church buildings or well-lighted parking lots; they have no Bible schools or seminaries; their leadership, such as it is, has no standing with the state, nor can disciples be promised prosperity, comfort and social acceptance. Yet in their daily associations, sharing with family and friends, meeting in homes or open fields to worship, directed by lay leaders trained in the school of life, and learning obedience through suffering, they are proving in our day that the apostolic pattern still works. When stripped of worldly power, and reduced to nothing but faith in God, then it seems that we get back to basics.

A Pattern for Us

This may partially explain why it is difficult to take Jesus' life-style seriously in an affluent, easy-going environment, though it can be done. The place to begin is with prayer. He tells us to pray for laborers to go into His harvest. To pray is to acknowledge that we are utterly insufficient in our own resources; yet, at the same time, it affirms that God is able to provide whatever is necessary. Any work we do for Him must issue from prayer, else it is an exercise in futility.

---

[6] I have heard these figures used by such recognized leaders as Thomas Wang, editor of *Chinese Around the World;* Philip Teng, President of the China Graduate School of Theology in Hong Kong; and James Taylor III, General Director of Overseas Missionary Fellowship, among others. An objective analysis of the church today in China by Leslie Lyall, *God Reigns in China* (London: Hodder and Stoughton, 1985).

In this dependence upon grace, we must take His servant's mantle, and sacrificially minister to the needs of people. Such concern will be understood and engender respect. One will never lack opportunity to disciple where practical love is manifest.

Those with a yearning to know Christ, a desire planted in the heart by God, should be noticed. It is likely such persons already have some affinity with us, which offers a point of introduction. I am convinced that a few such budding disciples are within the sphere of everyone's influence, beginning in the environs where we live and work.

With these learners we must find ways to get together as much as possible. The more natural the association, the better, like having dinner or playing ball. To give continuity to these casual gatherings, however, it may be helpful to structure some regular meetings in a small group. Occasionally times can be arranged for extended fellowship, perhaps going on a retreat. Of course, corporate meetings for worship and training in the local congregation will augment these more informal relationships.

A basic discipline can be accepted to encourage obedience. What is agreed on will depend upon the situation, but it might include daily devotions, Bible study and memorization, fasting or another form of abstinence, work in the church, visitation evangelism, social activities, or something else deemed important.

When together, we can show them how to minister. The emphasis is upon demonstration. They will catch on to our schedule of priorities, burdens of prayer, and way of witnessing in the context of living. This process will let them observe our failures and shortcomings, but let them also see a willingness to confess our sins and a readiness to make corrections.

Each learner can be involved in service according to his gifts. It is on-the-job training all the way. Everyone can do something. As faith and skills grow, their participation can enlarge. One way these learners can be utilized is in the follow-up of new believers. Incidentally, where this is practiced in the church, young converts need not ever be without a caring friend.

Faithfulness in completing tasks should be expected. So as we get back with disciples, we can ask them how they are coming along. When carnal attitudes surface, they should be rebuked. It will not be resented, if we are also astute in building self-esteem through affirmation and commendation. Remember, too, that whatever has been experienced thus far, there is more to discover in the infinite reaches of God's love.

In time learners will grasp our commitment to the Great Commission. Some of them may be able to enter doors of opportunity closed to us, perhaps even crossing a frontier never before penetrated with the gospel. Seed planted on prepared soil will bring forth fruit. As the process repeats itself in disciples, and they in turn do the same, our witness will continue to reach out in an ever-expanding circle to the ends of the earth and to the end of time.

The secret of the whole endeavor is to let the Spirit of Christ have His way. God's work cannot be done in the energy of the flesh. Only the indwelling Third Member of the Holy Trinity can produce the ministry of the Son. As this is realized, the life of Jesus becomes real; He lives and works through His disciples.

Misunderstandings of Discipleship

Obviously, not everyone understands discipleship this way. There are those who see it essentially as turning people to Christ and becoming members of the church.[7] Such a view clearly focuses the necessity of evangelism and church growth, but it leaves open development in the life-style of Jesus, leading to reproduction. Perhaps too much is made of the definition, but if making disciples of Christ does not result in men and women becoming disciplers, then the concept falls short of the scriptural pattern.

However, I can appreciate the position of these who equate disci-

---

[7] Church growth specialists, like Donald McGavran and Peter Wagner, generally use the term this way. They do not have any less concern for Christian nurture, called perfecting, but simply want to keep paramount the necessity of observable church extension. In technical categories, this discipling is given the designation D1 (a people turning to Christ from a non-Christian stance) or D2 (individual conversion), whereas D3 is the process of becoming a dedicated follower of Christ. A helpful clarification by Donald McGavran is "A 1979 Perspective on Church Growth," *The Asbury Seminarian,* XXXIV, (July, 1979), 3, pp. 6–13.

pleship with initial evangelism, for it preserves the indispensable element of bringing persons to Jesus.[8] Many churchmen have such an all-inclusive view of discipleship that the specific work of rescuing perishing souls from hell scarcely receives attention. Seeking to avoid this confusion of priorities, two decades ago when I wrote my book on principles of discipling in the life of Christ, it was entitled *The Master Plan of Evangelism.* I wanted to emphasize that evangelism is the cutting edge of the Great Commission and that invariably it will flow out of a Christian life-style.[9]

Where this is not understood, discipleship can be misleading, as some have observed.[10] Nevertheless, properly conceived and practiced, making disciples of the cross is the best way I know to heighten evangelistic concern in believers and to multiply the effective outreach of the whole body of Christ.[11]

---

[8] Carl Wilson contends that only in the last century did anyone think of the evangelistic enterprise as separate from discipling. Quoted in *Bulletin of Evangelical Ministries,* X, (March 1, 1983), 9, p. 1. Whether his view is correct or not, the point makes one stop and think.

[9] In recent years, there has been considerable material published on practical methods of personal discipleship. Authors who have written in the field include Walter A. Henrichsen, Leroy Eims, Gary Kuhne, Francis Cosgrove, Keith Phillips, Waylon Moore, John MacArthur, Allen Hadidian, J. Dwight Pentecost, Gene Warr, Carl Wilson, Billie Hanks, Jr., Doug Hartman, Doug Sutherland, William A. Shell, William MacDonald, Stephen Bly, Howard Snyder, Ronald Jenson, William Peterson, Lorne Sanny, Dan Crawford, Larry Richards, John Hendrix, Lloyd Householder, among others. Probably the best-known person in this field is the late Dawson Trotman, founder of the Navigators and long associate of Billy Graham. His little booklets: *Born to Reproduce* and *The Need of the Hour* (Colorado Springs: NavPress, 1957 and 1975) afford good introductions to this subject.

[10] In this regard, a perceptive observation is Bailey E. Smith's chapter "The Dangers of Deceptive Discipleship" in *Real Evangelism* (Nashville: Broadman, 1978), pp. 11-12. Though the author probably overstates the problem, and has an imbalanced view of discipling, still I recommend that students read his criticism.

[11] Church strategies emphasizing discipleship evangelism are being encouraged through many denominations, such as the Grade Ministry of the Wesleyan Church, the Into Construction Plan of the Church of the United Brethren in Christ, and the EvangeLife program of the Southern Baptists, to mention only a few. Among independent groups offering excellent programs are Churches Alive, Campus Crusade for Christ, International Evangelism Association, American Institute of Church Growth, Christian Outreach, and World Wide Discipleship Association.

A long look is needed—a projection of our witness to the next generation. I recognize that in the beginning the idea of concentrating on a few chosen people within our habitat may seem incompatible with the urgency to reach the world. What we dare not forget, however, is that laborers must be raised up for the harvest, which puts a premium upon equipping faithful men and women for the task.

Let no one fear that this process fosters a holier-than-thou mentality or creates a spiritual clique in the church. If this emerges, something is wrong. True discipleship is never an end in itself, nor can it be isolated from the larger Christian community. Everything done with the few is for the sake of Christ's mission to the world, the completion of which is for His praise alone.

It may be objected that such close association over a period of time smothers personality, and tends to make growing Christians dependent upon authority figures. The point is well taken if the discipler has an authoritarian manner. When this happens, the relationship can be counterproductive and should be terminated. Happily, though, Christ's discipling need not be so ordered. There is only one authority, the Word of God, finally revealed in Jesus Christ. Before Him, disciple and discipler alike must bow, and in this submission all grow toward the full stature of His character.

Let it be noted, too, that merely relating to people is no guarantee of success, anymore than every child raised in a Christian home will become a saint. Coming to Christ and maturing in His character is a personal choice, and no one can make the decision for another. Even one of Jesus' disciples turned out bad. Nevertheless, a fellowship of kindred spirits, just as a family, offers the most natural environment for learning.

But can't the institutional church provide this service? Why make the Great Commission a personal matter? It may be answered that the church does afford a congenial setting for discipleship, and the organization can do much to encourage it. Still the church functions through its members. To relegate the discipling of all nations to a congregation of people begs the question. Surely the church must fulfill the mandate, and that is precisely why every member of Christ's body is sent into the work.

Our Common Priesthood

More to the point, our Lord has given a model that all of us can
follow. Too easily we have assigned His ministry to those persons
who fit rather well-defined stereotypes of church work, like the
evangelist or Bible teacher. Sometimes it is even more narrowly limited to trained personnel who are properly ordained and commissioned for service. However, most people cannot identify with these
professional roles of ministry. For them the priesthood of all believers remains an elusive ideal. This is because ministry has been
equated with official church vocational callings, and not with the
more undergirding servant role of discipler.

The Great Commission comes as a corrective to this popular
misconception. In its focus upon life-style, our Lord's basic ministry
becomes a meaningful option to every child of God. The home-
maker, the farmer, the automobile mechanic in their natural sphere
of ministry have as much occasion to follow Christ's example as
does the renowned pastor or missionary. Some persons will have
special roles for which they are gifted, and their discipling will take
place through that calling.[12] But the Great Commission itself is not
a special gift or calling; it is an intentional daily servant life by
which teachable persons are led in the way of Christ. Since this is
best accomplished with a few people at a time, at least in depth relationships, everyone has about the same opportunity to make disciples. If this were more generally practiced, there would be a greater

---

[12] Take the specially gifted evangelist as an example. Because of his particular
calling, he may have opportunity to preach to thousands of people, of which
many may be converted to Christ. However, the effectiveness of his ministry is
largely dependent upon the faithful prayers and work of countless other persons
exercising different gifts. The evangelist's labor simply culminates their labors
in a decision, even as it fosters new demands for follow-up. Nevertheless, in his
personal life-style, with a few people close to him, the evangelist has the same
opportunity to disciple as the evangelist's wife, the evangelist's staff, or any
other member of the church. It may be difficult for an evangelist to keep this
basic personal ministry in focus, considering the pressure of larger evangelistic
endeavors, but it cannot be dismissed. One thing seems clear, if a popular evangelist can fulfill the Great Commission, then anyone can. I think that the personal life-style of Billy Graham, with his family and associates, is a good
illustration of how it can be done.

sense of true priesthood, church growth would soon overtake the expanding population, and the witness of Christ would go forth to every tribe and tongue and nation.

It comes down to an individual commitment. The responsibility to evangelize the world rests with every Christian. No one can be excused on the basis of not being gifted or called. For Jesus has made it quite clear that His discipling ministry is woven into the fabric of His life, and its ultimate objective, through the power of the Holy Spirit, is to bring God's good news to every creature.

Would it be fair to ask, where is our ministry being fulfilled in the making of disciples? Not that we have exclusive care of anyone, for thankfully other persons also impact with each life, and their faithfulness will have an effect, perhaps more than our own. Still we must ask ourselves, with a deliberative sense of mission, are we seeking to obey our Lord's command?

There can be no doubt that discipling is fraught with many dangers. But the difficulties must be weighed against the alternative. To neglect this ministry is more than disobedience; it is to retreat from the field of battle. It is, in effect. to abandon the mission of Christ by cutting the nerve of reproductive spiritual leadership.

This is not to suggest that discipling nullifies the need for preaching, teaching, healing, or any other aspects of Christ's ministry. Clearly these activities are essential to the work of His body. But undergirding them all and directing their fruitfulness is the life-style of the Great Commission.

This is the personal issue before us. How it is resolved ultimately will determine the relevance of our evangelism.

Questions for Thought

1. Why is the command to make disciples the secret of Jesus' plan to reach the unsaved with the gospel?

2. What makes one a disciple of Christ?

3. In what sense does the life and teaching of Jesus become the interpretation of the Great Commission? How can we follow His example today, considering the differences of our cultures, as well as the lapse of twenty centuries of time? What distinguishes an unchanging principle from a variable method?

4. How can it be said that the Great Commission is a life-style, not a special calling or gift of the Spirit?

5. What pitfalls should we seek to avoid in making disciples?

6. Why does every believer have about the same opportunity to fulfill the Great Commission?

10

Leadership for Evangelism in Theological Education

Walter C. Kaiser, Jr.

Walter C. Kaiser, Jr., is Professor of Old Testament and Se-
mitic Languages and Academic Dean and Vice President for
Education at Trinity Evangelical Divinity School. He came to
Trinity in 1964 after eight years of teaching at Wheaton College.
Ordained in the Evangelical Free Church, he has served as a pastor and maintains an active ministry in church conferences of
many denominations.

Based on his extensive speaking schedule, writings, and classroom experience, he has become an Evangelical spokesman for
Old Testament scholarship. Dr. Kaiser received the B.A. from
Wheaton College and the B.D. from Wheaton Graduate School
of Theology. His M.A. and Ph.D. were earned at Brandeis University.

A prolific author, scores of his articles have been published in
periodicals and scholarly journals. He has also written a number
of books, including *Classical Evangelical Essays in O.T. Interpretation; The Old Testament in Contemporary Preaching; Toward an
Old Testament Theology; Ecclesiastes: Total Life; Toward an Exe-
getical Theology: Biblical Exegesis for Preaching and Teaching; A
Biblical Approach to Suffering: Lamentations; Toward Old Testament Ethics; Malachi: God's Unchanging Love;* and *The Use of the
Old Testament in the New.*

Dr. Kaiser is a member of the Society of Biblical Literature and
a board member of the Near East Archaeological Society and
Wheaton College. In 1977, he served as national president of the
Evangelical Theological Society.

Modeling the Commission

The Great Commission must occupy the central focus of all Evangelical theological education. Without this lodestar in theological education, neither the church nor the academy will be successful. In fact, it is impossible to define the mission of the seminary (or related theological schools) without giving primary attention to the urgent command of the Lord of the church that men and women are to be trained to go into all the world to make disciples and to teach them all things He has commanded us.

Educators of the last two centuries have had a tendency to reverse the order of the priorities so clearly laid out in the Great Commission of Matthew 28:19–20. Such a reversal has led to an intellectualized and a purely academic approach to preparing leaders for the church. To be sure, high standards in the study and research of the biblical and theological curriculum must be maintained. But when these concerns become the heart of the enterprise, then our priorities have been inverted and we have begun to lose our motivation for carrying out our Lord's command.

In order to prevent this inversion of priorities and an overly affected academic approach to the preparation of men and women of God, special care must be taken to insure that a theological seminary gives strong leadership in this area of evangelism. Too frequently the academy has been content merely to acknowledge that there was a tension between the theoretical and nontheoretical aspects of the curriculum; or even more seriously, to tease about the practical and "impractical" subjects. But all such acknowledgments and teasings are more of an indictment of the contemporary way in which we carry out our theological task than anything else. The only proper way to address this situation is to expect that both sides of the academic aisle would immediately obligate themselves to carry out both types of theological tasks: the theoretical and practical. It is wrong for the seminary to expect her students to bridge this gap when they reach their parish or task in the church when these students have not observed the same principles operating in the seminary classroom or laboratory. Herein lies one of the great disadvantages of our overly specialized and fragmented curriculum.

While specialization in rather narrow fields of study has produced enormous gains both in the university and the seminary, it has not been without its attending losses. And in the case of the seminary it just cannot continue; for if it does, the heart and motivation for all Evangelical training will have been removed.

The education of a leader in the church begins and is maintained by following the same pattern inaugurated by the Lord of the church: teaching men and women how to make disciples. The academy must not feel that this is too childish or simplistic to engage the skills and interests of professionals who must earn their way among their scholarly peers in the more technical aspects of their own discipline. Instead, each professor must strive by example and by precept to relate the technicalities of his or her discipline to this central task. Only by first teaching our students how to make disciples will there then be a subsequent need to go on and teach these disciples. The trouble is that too many have become strictly didactic in their approach to the education of leaders. When this happens, the seminary has entered a quiescent period and is in danger of becoming obsolete.

Theme of Scripture

For those educators in the seminary who take the biblical text as their guiding instrument for a philosophy of education, it will be observed that the evangel has always been at the center of both testaments. Indeed, Genesis 12:3 already has recorded the heart of this concern in formulaic terms: "In your seed all the nations of the earth shall be blessed" (AT). This was the promise that provided the whole of Scripture—Old and New Testament—with its integrating center. In fact, the Apostle Paul exclaimed in Galatians 3:8 that what Abraham was being promised in Genesis 12:3 was the "gospel," that is, the evangel, itself. Accordingly, it is impossible to construct or do any Christian theology without locating the center of all biblical and theological concerns in this core. Moreover, this biblical center for theology is repeated so frequently in the text of Scripture that it is difficult to miss.

Not only is this promise to Abraham made the keystone of numerous texts between Genesis 12:3 and Galatians 3:8, but the same word is repeated and expanded to such ancient worthies as Isaac and Jacob, Moses and Joshua, David and Solomon, and to virtually everyone of the Davidic line of kings of Judah. Furthermore, this promise is captured in similar formulas such as appear almost fifty times in both treatments: "I will be your God; you shall be my people; and I will dwell in the midst of you" (for example, Exodus 29:45–46; 2 Corinthians 6:16; Revelation 21:3).

The puzzling fact is that the rumor persists that missions and evangelism were rather late developments. Especially frequent is the claim, which has almost become a byword, that the Old Testament was highly chauvinistic and nationalistic in its prejudice towards Israel without any concern for the evangelization of the nations, unless one sees a very late instance in the prophet Jonah and perhaps one or two other post-exilic writers. But such a view is unwarranted and contrary to the facts. God's plan from the very beginning of the Old Testament was universal and transnational, for Genesis 1–11 was directed to the whole family of nations listed in the table of nations in Genesis 10. And when the specific statement of the program of God is given to Abraham in Genesis 12:3, there is little left to the imagination.

To this great text must be added the equally wonderful moment when David realized that the promise God had just given to him was a renewal of that ancient word given to Abraham over a millennium ago, and he blurted out in happy exuberance: "This is the charter for mankind!" (see 2 Samuel 7:19). Likewise, the same can be claimed for another great moment in the text: "In that day I will restore the falling hut of David ... so that they may possess the remnant of Edom, even all the nations over which I will call my name" (see Amos 9:11–12).

It was this passage in Amos that provided the early church at the great Jerusalem Council with their basis for deciding that God had planned from ages ago that they indeed should have been faithful to the evangel of God's everlasting promise and that the promise included the Gentiles along with the Jews!

It would appear that our generation must learn the same lesson all over again. Neither the church nor its seminaries can rest on the laurels of its present company or success: that was the mistake of the

Jerusalem Church. Since it was unfamiliar with the plan of God in the Old Testament, it felt strange when God added to their number Gentiles who had responded to the missionary thrusts and evangelistic efforts of Paul and Peter. Must we be pushed by a revival into recovering the motivating center of theological education? Surely if leaders for the church are to be educated in this next decade, the seminary and academies of the church must reorganize their priorities and abilities to integrate the various specialties around this central and prior claim given by our Lord.

Problem of Pluralism and Universalism

Before we can consider a strategy for instituting evangelism in its proper place in theological education, it is necessary to raise some of the issues that tend to hamper the rightful place that evangelism should have in the preparation of leaders for the work of the ministry. Some of these issues have been treated already in the preceding chapters, but they will be listed here in order to capture the full picture and the difficulties faced by those who wish to restore evangelism to its central spot in the curriculum.

One is pluralism. This is not to say that there is no room for any diversity or difference of opinion; to the contrary, every provision must be made for that kind of pluralism which has an agreed upon biblical and theological unity. Notice we said unity not uniformity!

But a different state of affairs exists when the Dean of Yale University Divinity School must remonstrate: "Theological education . . . is characterized by the fact that there is virtually no substantive matter on which we agree. We [theological educators] are deeply, and sometimes polemically, divided over everything we think, believe and ought to do." He continued: "We are deeply divided . . . over how we understand the theological task. . . . We are even more deeply divided over the content of our theological work."[1]

Unfortunately there is all too much truth in this analysis. Of course many of our Evangelical schools will wish to deny the full

---

[1] Leander E. Keck, "Babel and Beyond," *Theological Education,* 21 (1984), 37–39.

measure of this application to their own situation, but if we fail to take full advantage of our name and likewise fail to incorporate the evangel itself as the great motivator for theological education, then we too shall ultimately deserve every last letter of that indictment! The issue of pluralism will not go away; it will only increase as we prepare for the twenty-first century.

A diversity in unity—but only in unity—is what is needed. We would urge the academy to a revitalized appreciation for the centrality of the Scriptures and the individual equipping of seminary students with a heart and passion for evangelism as the first and most significant step in the preparation of leaders.

Universalism is a related issue. All too frequently the claim is made these days that God will save the heathen by Himself, thank you, and that without our help or interference. Then comes a type of special pleading: God is a God of love and not a God who would condemn people to an eternal hell. Now while it is true that the anger of God never is explosive, unreasonable or borders on caprice, it is a rousing of His person to curb sin. There is not a hint of a desire for retaliation or a burning need to get revenge against those who have defied Him or who have refused all their lives to accept Him.

This charge is such an old canard that was faced already in the last half of the third century by the church Father Lactantius. He affirmed:

> He who loves the good by this very fact hates the evil; and he who does not hate the evil, does not love the good; because the love of goodness issues directly out of the hatred of evil, and the hatred of evil issues directly out of the love of goodness. No one can love life without abhorring death; and no one can have a appetency for light, without an antipathy to darkness.[2]

Therefore we find very little force in this drift towards universalism since it relies on a mistaken view of the nature of the love of God

---

[2] Lactantius, *De Ira Dei* in *The Minor Works,* transl. Sister Mary Francis McDonald, vol. 154 (Washington, DC: Catholic University of America Press, 1965), p. 69.

and weak view of the seriousness of man's lost estate apart from personally receiving the redeeming work of Christ. Unwittingly Evangelicals have also evidenced a practical kind of universalism when they fail to provide for a strong laboratory and classroom experience in evangelism and act as if they were embarrassed by its presence in the curriculum.

Other Problems

But the mood of modernity and the drift of evangelism in the preceding issues can now be matched with separatism, a preoccupation with the right wing of our theological brethren. It must be noticed that we have not said *separation,* for that is a biblical doctrine when rightfully explained; instead we have focused on separatism: the spirit and mentality that insist on having nothing whatsoever to do with anyone outside the family of faith, lest one become contaminated!

Such a super spirit of exclusivism can only lead to a new isolationism. What chance will there be for any meaningful exchanges, much less for the presentation of the gospel to those outside the family of God? The only point to be made in such separatism is that we don't really care that much for those for whom Christ died and in whom the image of God exists. Such religious snobbery is found both in the right and the left sides of the Evangelical theological spectrum. If the right refuses to develop friends among non-Christians, then the left refuses to share their faith actively and creatively out of fear that such might offend good taste. But the result is the same in that in both instances a watching world is robbed of the message of the Savior's love and gift of eternal life.

So significant is this last matter that the passion for respectability constitutes another barrier to evangelism. But what a high price to pay for the plaudits and esteem of scholarly peers and those outside the Evangelical orbit of influence! No one would make a case for ill-mannered or rude discourteousness as a Christian tactic no matter how high the goals were: the end cannot justify the means. Believers must always act with grace and tact, but tact must not rob zeal either! So it must be in the theological curricula. In this case the final accrediting association of our Lord is more to be respected than any worrying about whether the deliberate inclusion of evangelism in the seminary's list of courses will make it appear to be too much like the traditional layman's Bible school.

Another problem to face is the protestation that only a few have been given the gift of an evangelist. The way this excuse operates is a variation of the situation we have already described as operating on theological faculties. Everyone has a special calling or gift, goes the argument, and mine is not evangelism. All of this may be true, of course, but it will not change the terms of the Great Commission.

No doubt we do need to aim the seminary specifically at producing each year a number of gifted evangelists much as John Calvin purposed with his academy at Geneva. In our own situation at Trinity Evangelical Divinity School, I have asked our Lord to grant to us in each graduating class (currently with some 275 to 300 graduates each year) a minimum of five to seven itinerant evangelists and three to five teachers of evangelism. This is needful and a natural outcome of taking the Great Commission seriously.

But in no case should this ever become a substitute for involving the total leadership (and laity as well!) in the work of evangelism. Just because we have professionals to help us in mass meetings, chaplaincies, and the like does not mean that the whole task can be safely relegated to the pros. It is this same type of thinking that has led to the disciplinary isolation felt in the seminaries with its resulting loss of the motivational heart of teaching theology.

Every theological student should be given not only a textbook and classroom exposure to the discipline of evangelism, but also real, simulated and authentic opportunities for witness in the marketplace of the real world. It is difficult to see how our generation will ever accomplish the task of world evangelization unless every believer is involved. And how can we urge that everyone be involved if pastors and seminary professors are going to claim special exemptions under the unwritten rule of professionalism or some unstated shop rule of a special division of labor? The answer is obvious; therefore, we must urge the future leaders of all types in the church to receive the same advice that the Apostle Paul gave to young pastor Timothy: "Do the work of an evangelist" (2 Timothy 4:5 NIV). The point is inescapable, no matter which way we try to squirm out of it: our Lord enjoins us to disciple all peoples and the Apostle Paul prescribed it as one of the duties of the ministry.

The Need for Revival

It remains for us to describe some needed correctives for the future of Evangelical theological education. A good place to begin is with the need for a great awakening in our schools and among our pastors. The current situation, if the truth be told, is close to what Charles Finney described in another day. He bluntly asserted:

> ... Ministers ought to know that nothing is more common than for spiritual Christians to feel burdened and distressed at the state of the ministry. ... When a minister has gone with a church as far as his experience in the spiritual goes, there he stops; and until he has a renewed experience, ... his heart is broken afresh, and he sets forward in the Divine life and Christian experience, he will help them no more. He may preach sound doctrine, and so may an unconverted minister; but, after all, his preaching will want that searching pungency, that practical bearing, that unction which alone will reach the case of a spiritually minded Christian. It is a fact over which the Church is groaning, that the piety of young men suffers so much in the course of their education, that when they enter the ministry, however much intellectual furniture they may possess, they are in a state of *spiritual boyhood.* They want nursing; they need rather to be fed, than to undertake to feed the Church of God.[3]

Probably the greatest need for revival today is in our seminaries. In fact, how can we even begin to adequately prepare men and women as leaders in the church unless there is a fresh anointing of the Holy Spirit upon the lives of those who teach, administer and who are taught?

---

[3] Charles G. Finney, *Revivals of Religion* (Old Tappan, NJ: Revell, n.d.), pp. 126–7.

Holiness of life is not spiritual luxury that we may wish to add or delete depending on the current state of our feelings. And nowhere does this show up more forcibly than in the teaching of evangelism. No longer can there be any questions about the fact that concern for spiritual formation in the life of the theological student is just as important as the finest development for one's biblical and theological skills and methodologies. Included in any list of significant spiritual exercises is the word: "He that wins souls is wise" (Proverbs 11:30 NIV). Therefore we urge that evangelism be added to those curricula that still list it only as an elective course or that do not list it at all. We also urge that it be given top priority and that it be taught by some of the most able and convincing faculty members who are able to lead the class by example as well as precept. It should also stress the essential connection between the witness's spiritual preparation and the effectiveness of that witness.

Facing the Challenge of a Lost World

The task will never be larger or more challenging than it will be over the next fifteen years. In this short decade and a half the world population will almost double from the dizzy heights of its present total of 4.7 billion to almost 7 billion by the year 2000 A.D. if our Lord tarries. That would mean that the church must double every existing parish, institution, mission station, parachurch ministry almost immediately. And this comes precisely at the moment when the number of potential, first-career recruits graduating from our universities, colleges, and Bible schools and colleges will hit its lowest trough in 1990—the lowest number of graduates since the high reached in 1975.

Obviously the church has its work cut out for it if we take seriously the fact that all the people of the world are lost until they receive the Savior. But how shall they hear if no one goes to tell them the good news? This is no time for passivity or neutrality. The seminary must stand up and be counted. What is more, it must be in the vanguard leading the church if she is to be worthy of the inestimable amount of goodwill, trust and finances that have been poured into her.

Should the seminaries fail at this critical moment in history, there will be more serious consequences than the *Ichabod* that will be written over her gates. We will have missed one of earth's finest hours in the program of God; yes, finest because never was so much committed to so few with such great resources and with such epic proportions of promise in terms of results. In many ways it is as if this is what we in theological education have been planning for all along. Now comes the most critical test of the effectiveness of the church's academy.

The Waiting Multitudes Overseas

To face the staggering odds noted in the coming human wave is to raise another needed corrective: a need for a new strategy of proportionality. Can theological schools afford the luxury of thinking and planning as if 60 to 70 percent of their graduates will assume North American pastorates while the great increases in population take place in the third world and among those areas that contain hidden peoples who remain among the vast number of the unreached?

We think not. It is high time that those institutions that like to feel that they are presenting the most advanced and best training available for long-range service in the church take the lead in sending as many of their graduates into making disciples of these nations as they send to teach the churches of North America.

This is not to say that the job in America has neared completion. By no means is this so. On the contrary, we must attack the task of planting new churches much more aggressively than we ever have before. We at Trinity have, therefore, inaugurated a new church planting major with an in-service component along with special scholarships and course work. Furthermore, our sponsoring denomination, the Evangelical Free Church of America has been planting churches in America recently at the rate of one new church per week. But all of this, impressive as it might seem, is still miniscule in comparison to the size of the task facing the church.

Nevertheless, having acknowledged all this does not subtract one bit from the gargantuan size of the task facing us in Europe and the third world. Seminaries must urge that at least as many graduates assume their roles as witnesses overseas as assume their roles in the States and Canada.

For too long the church has had to rely on Evangelical schools that typically provided a one-year basic orientation to the Scriptures as the chief sources for the majority of our missionary staff presently serving around the world. For this we in the Evangelical church stand in their debt and offer our deep thanks to the Lord of the church for raising up these schools.

Times have changed, however, and we have witnessed a most unusual phenomenon during these last twenty years: the rise and unprecedented expansion of the Evangelical seminary movement. Given the complicated nature of communicating cross-culturally and with the need for equipping the national churches around the world for ministry in a day filled with new levels of political and educational sophistication, it is time that the seminary movement gave a good accounting of itself to the Lord of the church.

We urge therefore that evangelism be taught not only for the needs of North America, but with a view to sharing Christ across every cultural, linguistic, ethnic, political, and religious barrier. We urge that new strategies and methods be devised for reaching groups of peoples who have been notoriously difficult to reach for Christ. We urge that such strategies be tested out in the great cities and urban centers of America to whose doorsteps have come the nations of the world either for relief or for an education. If the church cannot demonstrate that it is capable of penetrating the cities for Christ here in America, how will a plane ride for a new missionary change anything?

Taking the Offensive

A final corrective might be noted. We need to search both from the Holy Spirit and from those tools the Spirit has already placed in our hands, for a new awareness of how we can make our appeal to men and women apart from Christ.

We would urge the church into the posture of an aggressive offensive. What with the power of the resurrection and the presence of the indwelling Christ, not to mention the authority of the Scriptures, it is almost inconceivable that the church exhibits in so many parts of the world such anemic results and present status. Surely God has gifted the church somewhere with a contemporary version of Paul or Barnabas! Surely with all the gifted brains and the large reservoir of workers and leaders we should be able to come up with more innovative methods for accomplishing the age-old task of being a light to the nations.

Our inertia may be due to many factors. Some of us have been frightened away from maintaining any standards of academic excellence in carrying out the challenge of evangelizing our generation. Others have been loathe to recognize the freedom of the Spirit of God in using "charismatic" versus "official" models for evangelism. Others have been hampered by a failure to develop an active discipleship through the training process and thereby standing alongside the student both in encouragement and prayer. Others have not sensed the importance of motivating students and future leaders to do the work of evangelism, for everything in their body is pointing in the opposite direction when they go to witness for Christ. Furthermore, a "cool" generation has spread its gospel that the kindest gesture anyone could do for another person is "to live and let live," that is, in the vernacular, "don't bug them." No wonder great encouragement is needed and an active program of active discipleship *in situ* is essential.

By now our case is clear. The seminary must take the lead in providing the most original, most spiritually sensitive, most creative discipleship program in evangelism the church or world has ever witnessed. This could well be the finest hour that the church of Jesus Christ has ever experienced.

We urge the theological leadership around the world to demonstrate a high priority and commitment to the task of evangelism. We urge that petty jealousies and the party spirit and denominational barriers be dropped and replaced with a new appeal to God for a mighty outpouring of His Spirit. May the Lord of the harvest graciously aid us in accomplishing this task, not as though we had anything to claim in ourselves; rather that in our weakness we can be strong for "our competence comes from God" (2 Corinthians 3:5 NIV).

Questions for Thought

1. In what ways could the preparation of theological leaders be strengthened so as to order our priorities in accordance with those of the Great Commission?

2. What great personages and passages from the Bible come to mind as you move from Genesis to Revelation on the "promise-plan" theme of the gospel?

3. If you were in charge of formulating a strategy for the church worldwide, how would you suggest that we immediately act to finish the task of evangelizing the world?

4. What impediments do you and your friends face when it comes time to witness for Christ and what have the Scriptures told us are God's answers for each particular obstacle we can raise?